IMAGES
of America
SOUTHERN
ST. JOSEPH COUNTY

IMAGES
of America

SOUTHERN
ST. JOSEPH COUNTY

Franklin N. Sheneman II

ARCADIA

Published by Arcadia Publishing,
Charleston SC, Chicago IL, Portsmouth NH, San Francisco CA.

Printed in Great Britain.

Library of Congress Catalog Card Number: 2004104905

For all general information contact Arcadia Publishing at:
Telephone 843-853-2070
Fax 843-853-0044
E-Mail sales@arcadiapublishing.com
For customer service and orders:
Toll-Free 1-888-313-2665

Visit us on the internet at http://www.arcadiapublishing.com

In memory of my father, Dale Sheneman, and in honor of my mother Kathie Sheneman.

CONTENTS

ACKNOWLEDGMENTS

A book such as this is more a collaborative effort than the work of the author alone. Therefore I wish to express my heartfelt apperception to the following people. First and foremost to the many individuals, families, groups, and organizations that supplied their photographs and shared their memories. Without you, this book would simply not exist. To my editor, Samantha Gleisten, who was always available to answer any questions I had. To John Kovach for his thoughtful advice and technical skills. To all of my friends at the St. Joseph County Public Library for their words of encouragement. To Janet Rhodes and Chuck and Marilyn Sherland for opening the Walkerton Area Historical Society's Heritage House during off hours so that I could scan photographs and conduct research. To four of the most important people in my life; Emily Klinedinst, Karin Stevens, Becca VanWechel, and Sharon Zechowski, your laughter, friendship, and support means more to me than you will ever know. And finally I wish to dedicate this book in memory of my father, Dale Sheneman, and in honor of my mother Kathie Sheneman for all that they have done for me and for teaching me to be proud of my rural roots.

INTRODUCTION

It is hard to imagine when traveling through Southern St. Joseph County that at one time the landscape was nothing more than a sheet of ice with prehistoric mammals such as gigantic mammoths strolling through the very lands where homes stand today. Or that less than 200 years ago, Potawatomi Indians farmed and hunted alongside pioneer settlers. What isn't so hard to imagine is the hardworking pioneering spirit and strong sense of community our ancestors had, for it still exists to this day.

The history of Southern St. Joseph County is as rich as the fertile lands that brought the first residents here in the 1830s. The county itself was officially recognized by the state of Indiana on April 1, 1830. The first township in the southern part of the county to be established was Greene Township, which was named for John Greene who settled upon Sumption Prairie in 1832. The township was officially formed on January 4, 1836. Other families to follow were the Garwood, Rupe, Ort, Reaves, Hummer, Hammond, and Cook families. The next of the southern townships to be formed was Union on March 6, 1837. Among the first settlers there were the Lineback, Henderson, Riddle, Moon, Lamb, and Lon families, to name but a few. Liberty Township was the next township to be formed on May 2, 1837. Five years prior to the establishment of the township, the following families settled in the area: Rupel, Earhart, Liggett, Cole, Pearce, Cripe, Palmer, and Williams. On March 4, 1845 the township of Madison became the next township to be located in Southern St. Joseph County. Unlike previously populated townships, Madison Township did not see settlers there until the 1840s. Among the first pioneer families were the Kline, Kiefer, Bennett, Helminger, Marker, Newcomer, Birk, and Fox families. Lincoln Township was formed on June 7, 1866 as disgruntled residents of southern Liberty Township were tired of crossing swampy grounds to vote in North Liberty. Although at the time part of Liberty Township, the first settlers of the area that would later become Lincoln Township were the Fulmer, Wiley, Ruggles, Cole, Barton, Usher, and Frost families.

Of the three incorporated towns in Southern St. Joseph County, North Liberty was the first to be established on January 12, 1836 by Daniel Antrim. Named for John Walker, who brought the Indianapolis, Peru and Chicago Railroad to the area, the town of Walkerton was platted on June 20, 1856. Once merely a resting point for weary travelers on route to Lake Michigan from the Ohio River, the town of Lakeville saw a great boom at the turn of the 20th century and was officially incorporated on July 7, 1902.

This book is by no means meant to be a comprehensive collection of the history of Southern St. Joseph County but rather a reflection of the hardworking, rural lifestyle that has shaped over 170 years worth of memories. Each chapter is devoted to aspects of the community that I feel represent the ideologies held dear to people in this area, with the final chapter being a comparison of images of yesterday to those of today. If I've learned one thing in gathering the vintage photographs for this book, it's that the strong sense of community and pride that has been passed down from our ancestors will continue to transcend the test of time to future generations of Southern St. Joseph County.

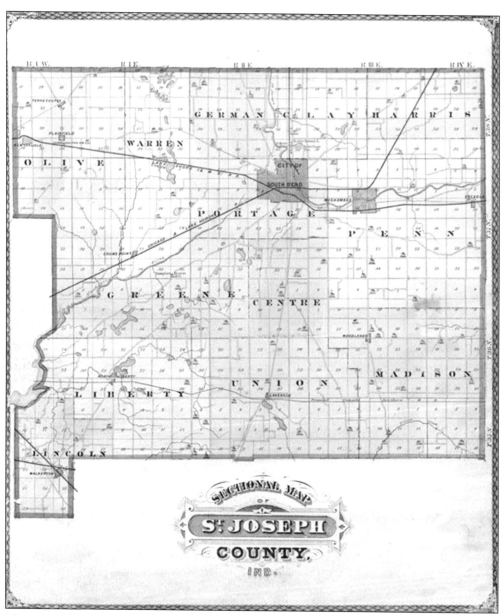

This map shows St. Joseph County as it appeared in the year 1875. While the towns of South Bend and Mishawaka continued to expand and grow into cities, little has changed in the towns in the southern part of the county. Lakeville, North Liberty, and Walkerton have been able to maintain their tranquil and rural charm throughout the years. (From the collection of the St. Joseph County Public Library.)

One

FAMILY

"The root of the kingdom is in the state. The root of the state is in the family. The root of the family is in the person of its head."

—Mencius

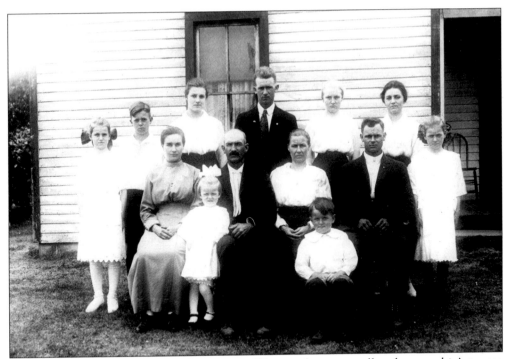

Charles Naragon of Liberty Township was a well known farmer as well as the township's trustee in the early 1920s. Mr. Naragon and his wife, Sarah (Stull) pose with their family on their farm c. 1915. Pictured from left to right are: (front row) Vera, Marie, Mr. Naragon, Mrs. Naragon, Raymond, Russell, Dora; (back row) Helen, Howard, Mary, Lee, Frieda, and Ester. (From the collection of Debra Futa.)

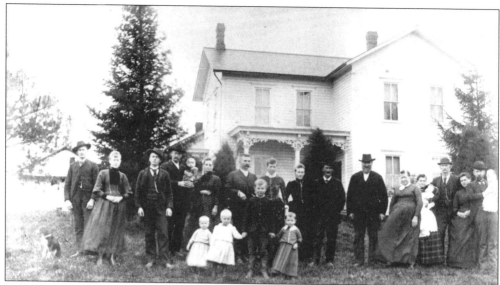

Members of the Americus and Sarah (Ogborn) Bunch family of Lakeville pictured in this 1890 photograph are: (front row) Floyd, Warren, Bert Lee, Cecil; (back row) George, Laura Alice, Rollo Elmer, Charles Albert, Flora (Walz), Andrew Krieger, Leana May, Adeline, John Phillips, Mr. Bunch, Mrs. Bunch, Lillian Merrill, Clyde, William, Emma Kern, Harrison Walter Bunch. (From the collection of Eileen Copsey.)

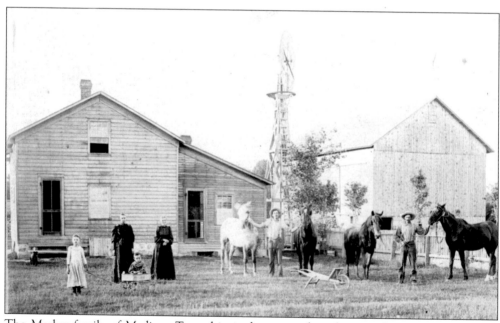

The Marker family of Madison Township is shown on their farm in this 1901 photograph. Pictured, from left to right, are: Nora Marker, Mary (Mason) Marker, Delbert Marker, Barbara (Besler) Mason, farm hand Chas Keil, and Fred Marker. (From the collection of Peggy Marker.)

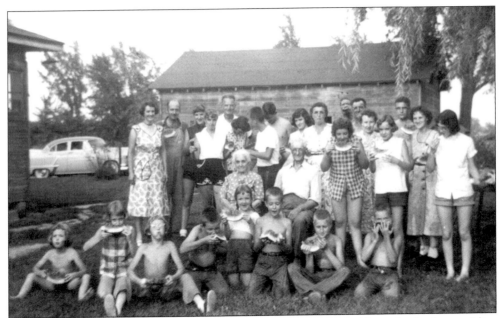

Enjoying a hot summer day with their family are John Olinger Jr. and his wife, the former Alice Steele. Mr. Olinger was part owner and manager of the Lakeville Lumber Company, as well as a member of both the town and school boards. He and his wife are the first two individuals in the second row c. 1955. (From the collection of Gloria Kingery.)

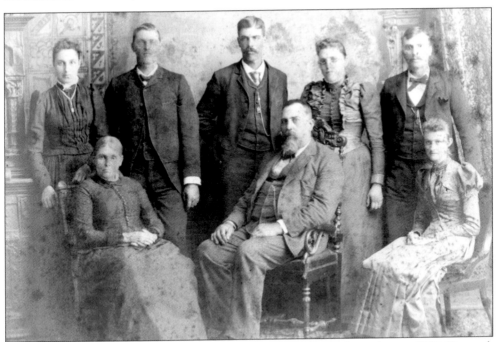

The family of Levi and Sarah (Houser) Knepp of North Liberty is shown here c. 1880. Pictured, from left to right, are: (front row) Mrs. Knepp, Mr. Knepp, Laura (Knepp) Mangus; (back row) Angie (Price), Jonathan D., George F., Fairy, and Albert Mangus. (From the collection of Gladys Albright.)

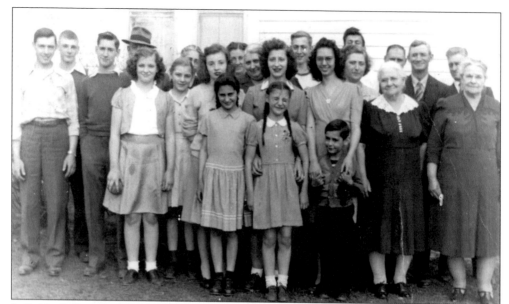

Individuals that grew up near Pine Creek are shown in this 1944 photo. Pictured here, from left to right, are: (front row) Lucy Clark, Susie Liggett Jim Clark; (second row) Lucille Liggett, Carolyn Judd, Margaret Judd, Jenny Liggett, Joyce Clark, Anna Steele, Ella Houser; (back row) Keith Clark, Maurice Liggett, Don Clark, Herman Judd, Hazel Clark, Mary Judd, Robert Judd, Lloyd Clark, Sarah Judd, George Clark, Bernice Liggett, and Marvin Judd. (From the collection of Joyce Halt.)

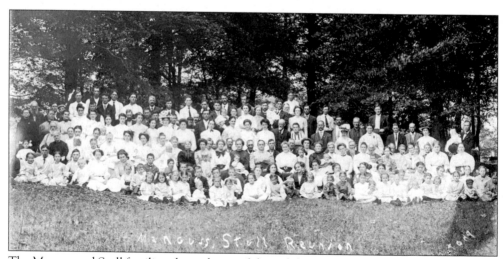

The Mangus and Stull families, shown here, celebrated their annual reunion in this shady grove in 1910. (From the collection of Gladys Sheneman.)

Fredrick Schrader, born in Germany in 1857, one of the most renowned carpenters in the entire county, stands in front of the majestic home he built in Liberty Township. (From the collection of Delores Anderson.)

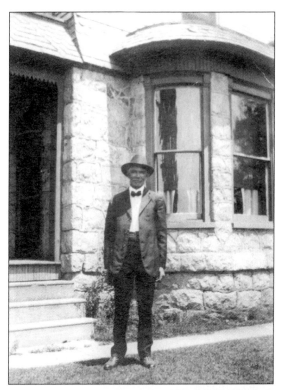

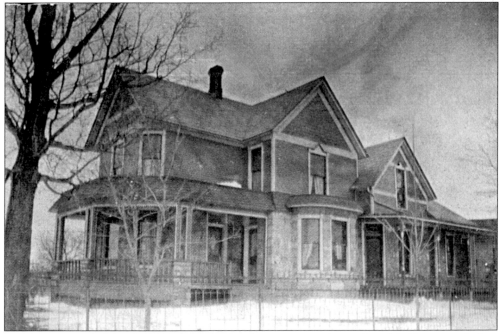

Four generations of the Fredrick Schrader family grew up in the multi-gabled home including the families of his daughter Mabel (Schrader) Anderson and the family of his grandson, Herb Anderson. The house still stands today, south of North Liberty on State Road 23. (From the collection of Delores Anderson.)

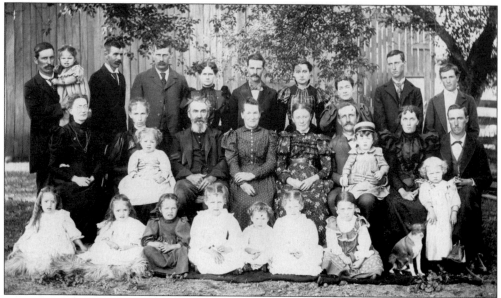

Mr. and Mrs. Michael Steele, middle row center, are shown with their family in Liberty Township c. 1898. (From the collection of Joanne Carter.)

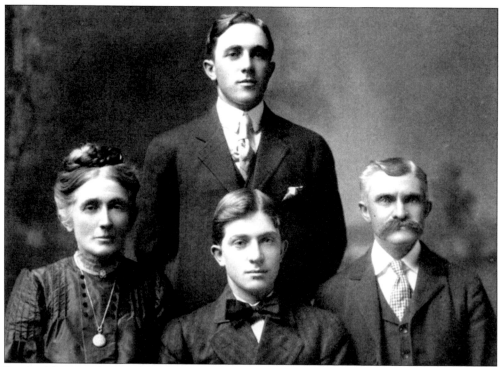

Pictured here in this c. 1907 photograph is the family of Henry Smith. In 1878, Mr. Smith married Anastasia Dare. Their oldest son Leonard taught at the Walkerton High School and later graduated from the University of Notre Dame with a degree in civil engineering. Pictured, from left to right are: Mrs. Smith, Henry Myron, Mr. Smith; (back row) Leonard. (From the collection of the St. Joseph County Public Library.)

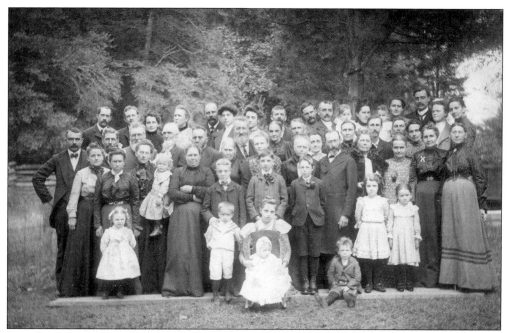

Seen here is the Price family of Liberty Township c. 1900. (From the collection of Gladys Albright.)

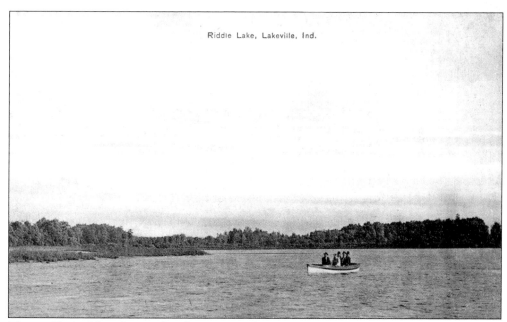

Riddle Lake, Lakeville, Ind.

The popular Riddle Lake in Lakeville was named after Henry Riddle. When Mr. Riddle purchased the land in 1836 it included a portion of the lake. It has bared his name ever since. A group of people enjoy a leisurely boat ride on the lake c. 1915. (From the collection of Toni Cook.)

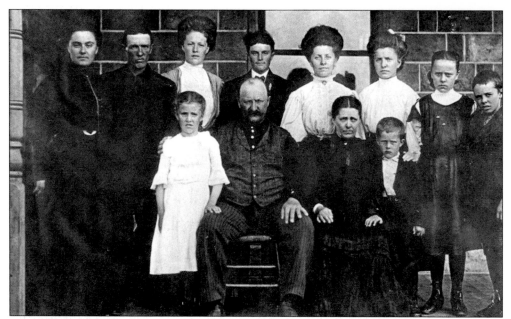

The family of William and Katie (Kaser) Nelson stand on the front porch of the family home, which was located on the corner of Osborne and Smilax Roads in Liberty Township c. 1910. Pictured, from left to right, are: (front row) Minnie, Mr. Nelson, Mrs. Nelson, Melvin; (back row) Verna, Howard, Hazel, Jean, Nellie, Carrie, Edna, and Bob. (From the collection of Verla Burgener.)

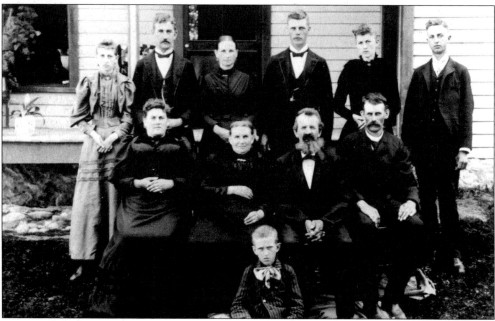

The Walz family of Union Township poses in front of the family home during the summer of 1894. Seated, from left to right, are: Anna, Sophia (Mainer), John, and Charles. Standing, left to right, are: Ida, Christian, Flora, George, Amelia, and John. The youngest member of the family, Fred, sits on the ground in front of his family. (From the collection of Eileen Copsey.)

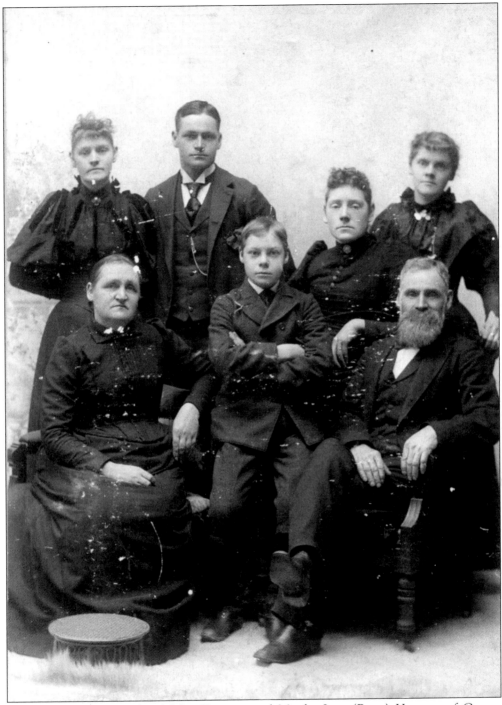

Shown here is the family of John Hummer and Martha Jane (Rupe) Hummer of Greene Township, *c.* 1890. Pictured from left to right are: Mrs. Hummer, Harrison Wade, Mr. Hummer; (back row) Myrtle, John Alva, Cena, and Ella. Mrs. Hummer's grandfather, Jacob Rupe, was among the first pioneer settlers of Greene Township in 1840. Mr. Hummer's father, Washington, came from Ohio a few years later. (From the collection of the author.)

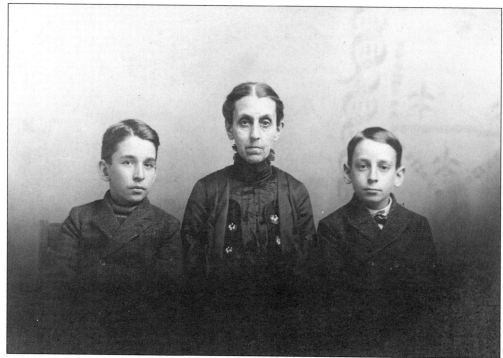

Vivian and Maurice Fitzgerald pose with their grandmother, Elizabeth Platz in this late 19th-century photograph. (From the collection of the Walkerton Area Historical Society.)

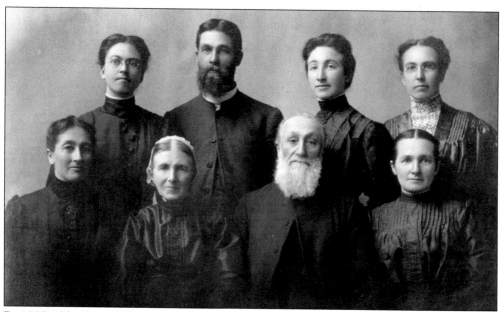

By 1925, Elder Daniel Whitmer had served the longest in the ministry of the Brethren Church in all of Indiana. Members of his family are shown in this *c.* 1900 photograph. From left to right, they are: (front row) Emmie Hartman Grammer, Elizabeth (Inman) Whitmer, Elder Daniel Whitmer, Elzina Rupel; (back row) Elvie Miller, M.I. Whitmer, Margaret Stutsman, and Rosie Whitmer. (From the collection of Debra Futa.)

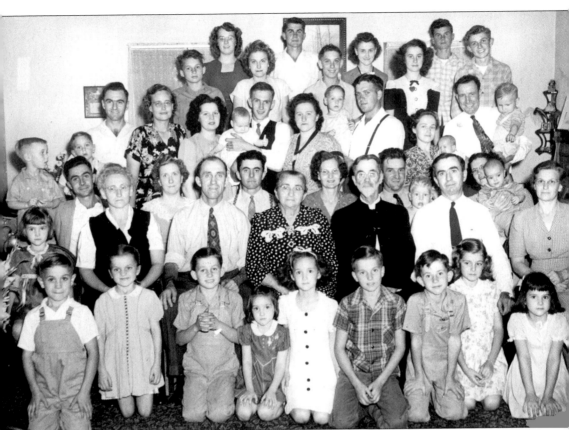

Members of the Meril I. and Lillie (Clark) Whitmer family gather in the Whtimer's home in the fall of 1946 to celebrate the couple's 50th wedding anniversary. Members of the family, pictured left to right, are: (front row) Paul Dean Whitmer, Linda Whitmer, Bert Whitmer, Paulette Olinger, Elaine Olinger, Rollo Whitmer, Jerry Whitmer, Barbara Whitmer, Christie Olinger; (second row) Sharon Olinger, Grace Whitmer, M.D. Whitmer, Mrs. Whitmer, Mr. Whitmer, Richard Whitmer, Helen Whitmer; (third row) Philip Whitmer, Paul Whitmer, Katherine Whitmer, Inman Whitmer, Dora Whitmer, Paul Olinger, John Olinger, Bernice Olinger, Daniel Olinger; (forth row) Merlin Whitmer, David Whitmer, Lela Whitmer, Donna Whitmer, John Whitmer, Shirley Whitmer (baby), Margaret Davis, Johnny Davis, Jim Davis, Agnes Gorby, Phyllis Gorby, Claude Gorby, Jerry Gorby; (back row) Jim Whitmer, Josephine Whitmer, Martha Whitmer, Charles Whitmer, David Whitmer, Alice Whitmer, Evelyn Whitmer, Eugene Whitmer, Duane Whitmer. (From the collections of Gloria Kingery and Margaret Davis.)

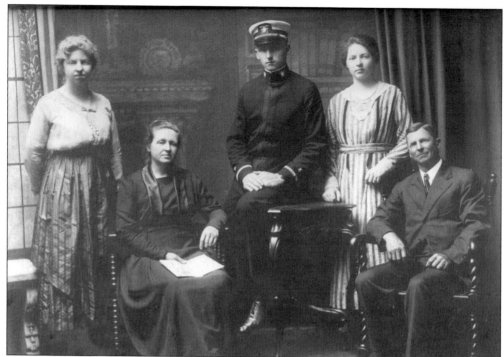

William Orlando Cullar was a well-known farmer as well as a highly respected teacher in Southern St. Joseph County. His stately family farm was located on Oak Road. The family gathered for this photo, taken at the time of World War I. Pictured, from left to right, are: Eva, Mrs. Mary (Barrett) Cullar, Fred Orlando (a veteran of WW I), Nell, and Mr. Cullar. (From the collection of Joanne Carter.)

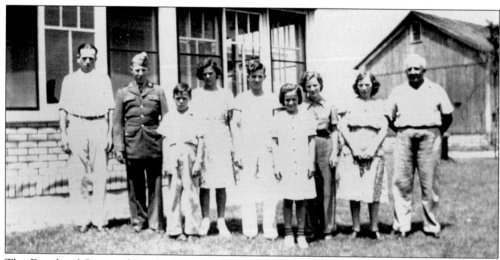

The Family of Otto and Bertha Mae (Walter) Schmeltz stand in front of the family home on Walnut Road in Lincoln Township. Pictured in this photograph taken July of 1941, from left to right, are: Virgil, Linder, Ralph, Violet Mae, Arthur, Wanda Lea, Evelyn Lucille, Mrs. Schmeltz, and Mr. Schmeltz. (From the collection of Randy Schmeltz.)

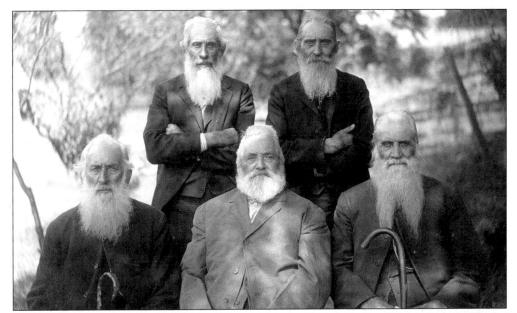

Like many pioneer families in Liberty Township, the Sheneman family's ancestry is that of "Pennsylvania Deutsch." After arriving in the U.S. from Germany, a large population of Germans settled in Pennsylvania before moving to Ohio and later Indiana. Pictured in this c. 1911 photograph, from left to right, are brothers: (front row) Fred, Henry, Isaac; (back row) Zakarius and John. (From the collection of Gladys Sheneman.)

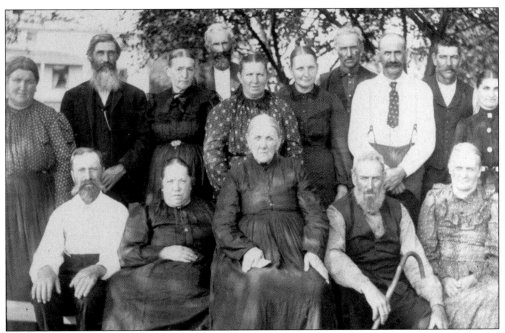

Born on August 10, 1823, Susanna (Stump) Newcomer was another sturdy pioneer women who traveled from state to state before calling Southern St. Joseph County home. Mrs. Newcomer sits, front row center, with her children and their spouses at a family reunion in 1905. (From the collection of Sandra Jane Harman.)

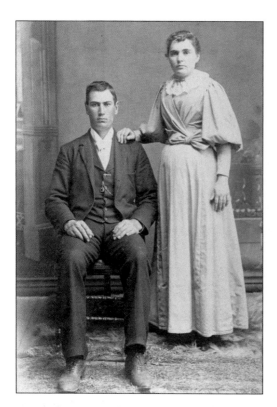

Ed McDaniel and his wife Mina (Beatty) are seen here around the time of their weeding, which took place on May 14, 1896. Mr. McDaniel was a farmer in Lincoln Township. (From the collection of the Walkerton Area Historical Society.)

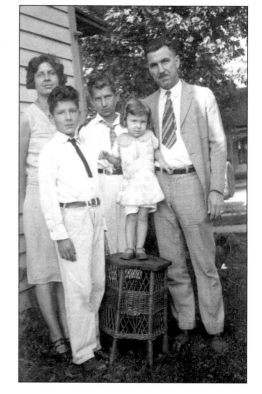

E.P. McDaniel was well known throughout the town of North Liberty as the local undertaker. Members of the McDaniel family pictured here c. 1930, from left to right, are: Francis, Gail, Earl, Fauntelle, and Mr. McDaniel. (From the collection of Fauntelle Spellman.)

Myron LeRoy and his son Worth of Walkerton pose for this studio photograph in the late 1800s. (From the collection of the Walkerton area Historical Society.)

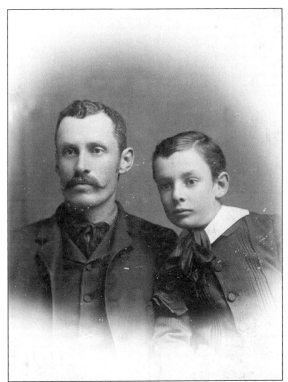

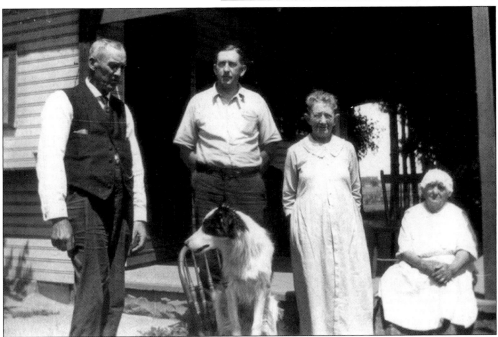

The LeRoy family was known throughout Walkerton for their entrepreneurial spirit. William Stephen Leroy also delivered mail with a horse drawn carriage. Pictured in this *c.*1925 photograph, from left to right, are: William, Faunt, Elizabeth (Pommert), and Otilla (Honer) Pommert. (From the collection of Eric Nelson.)

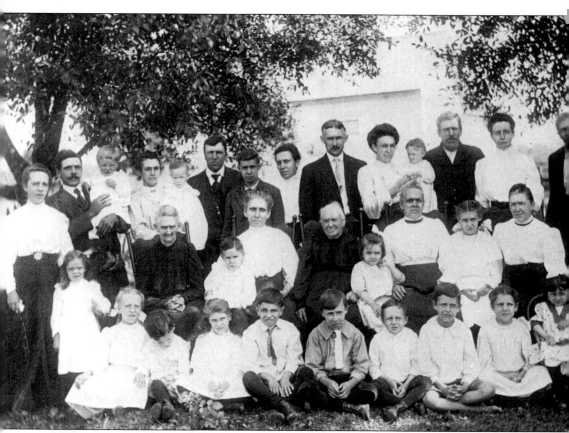

The family of William and Elizabeth (Oberholtzer) Kaser pose on the family farm located on Pine Road just south of Quinn, c. 1910. Pictured, from left to right, are: (front row) Lela Kaser, Ralph Kaser, Ida Sholly, Cloise Oberholtzer, Franklin Sholly, Gail Oberholtzer, Vernon Kaser, Ethel Kaser, Helen Oberholtzer; (second row) Cass Newcomer, Charles Kaser, Alice Kaser, Mrs. Kaser, Hattie Oberholtzer, Sarah Sholly, Ada Sholly, Mary Kaser; (back row) Lela Kaser, Ralph Kaser, Ida Sholly, Closie Oberholtzer, Franklin Sholly, Gail Oberholtzer, Vernon Kaser, Ethel Kaser, Helen Oberholtzer. (From the collections of Deborah Morgan and Elmer Sholly.)

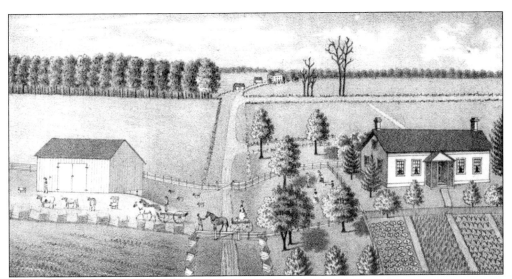

The Barrett Farm, located in Union Township, was typical of a small country farm in 1875. (From the Collection of the St. Joseph County Public Library.)

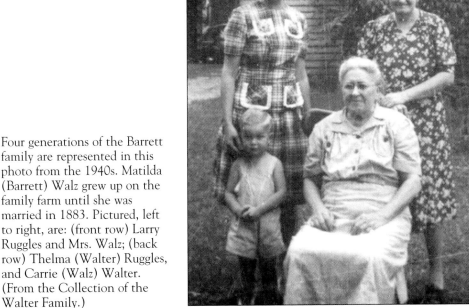

Four generations of the Barrett family are represented in this photo from the 1940s. Matilda (Barrett) Walz grew up on the family farm until she was married in 1883. Pictured, left to right, are: (front row) Larry Ruggles and Mrs. Walz; (back row) Thelma (Walter) Ruggles, and Carrie (Walz) Walter. (From the Collection of the Walter Family.)

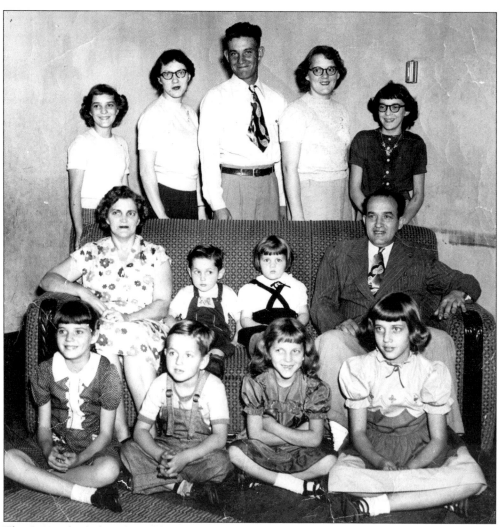

The Ivo and Thelma (Smith) Peddycord family of North Liberty are shown here c. 1952. Pictured, from left to right, are: (front row) Betty, John, June, Carol; (middle row) Mrs. Peddycord, Michael, Jennifer Jo, Mr. Peddycord; (back row) Fudge, Loetta, Milo, Joyce, and Nancy. (From the collection of Betty Peddycord.)

Two
FARM LIFE

"When tillage begins, other arts follow. The farmers therefore are the founders of human civilization."

–Daniel Webster

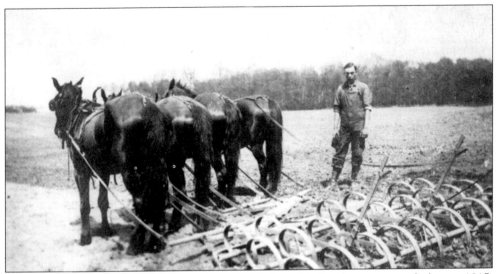

This farmer from Greene Township takes a break from his four horse powered plow *c.* 1917. (From the collection of the author.)

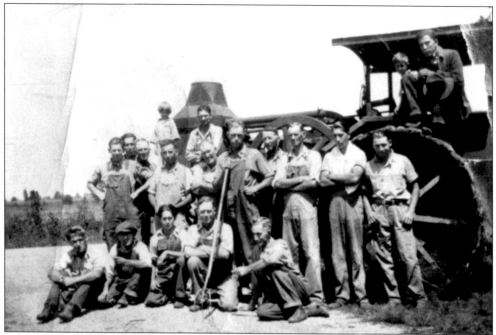

In 1932, a group of farmers take a break from the fields to pose for this picture. Farmers there that day included (in no particular order); George Matz, Pauline Matz, Leroy Matz, Claude Watkins, Finley Patterson, Walter Kaiser, Howard Brown, Russell Skiles, Bill Schultz, Orville Buss, Clifford Skiles, and Herschel Holenbaugh. (From the collection of the Walkerton Area Historical Society.)

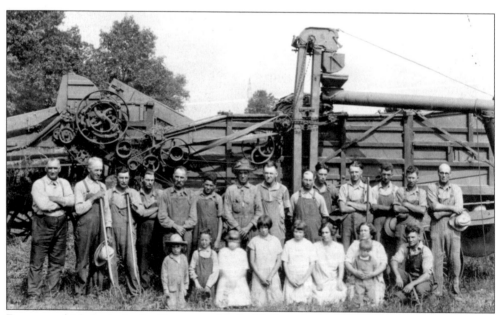

Farmers, which include the Pippenger, Nash, Mullett, Lowry, Stienke, Snyder, and Thayer families, pose on the Pippenger farm outside of Walkerton in August of 1925. (From the collection of the Walkerton Area Historical Society.)

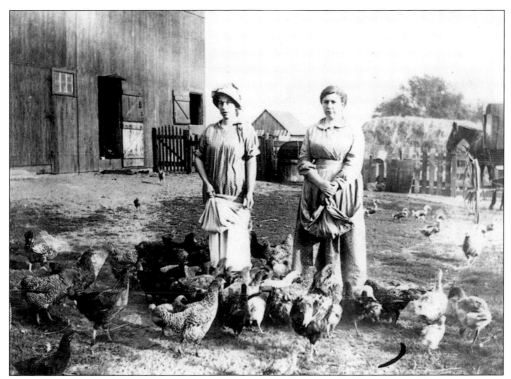

Sisters Nellie and Grace Hahn collect eggs on the family farm near Walkerton. (From the collection of the Walkerton Area Historical Society.)

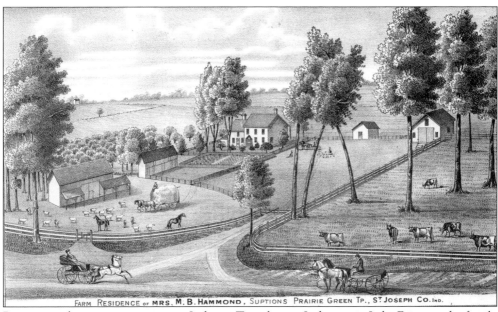

FARM RESIDENCE of MRS. M. B. HAMMOND, SUPTIONS PRAIRIE GREEN TP., ST. JOSEPH CO. IND.

Pioneers took many routes to get to Indiana. Traveling to Indiana, via Lake Erie, was the family of Matthew B. Hammond. Mr. Hammond was one of the first settlers of the county to purchase land in the area of Greene Township known as Sumption Prairie. The Hammond farm is shown here in this 1875 sketch. (From the collection of the St. Joseph County Public Library.)

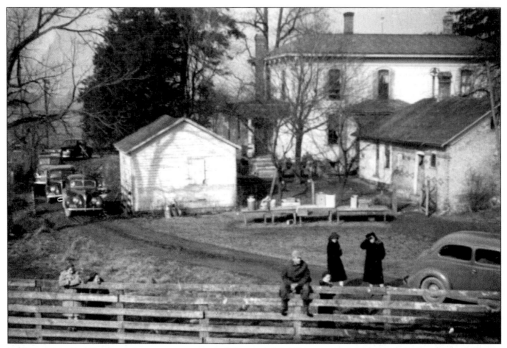

Selling the family farm is never an easy thing to do. The auction of the Marker Family farm took place on February 20, 1943. (From the collection of Peggy Marker.)

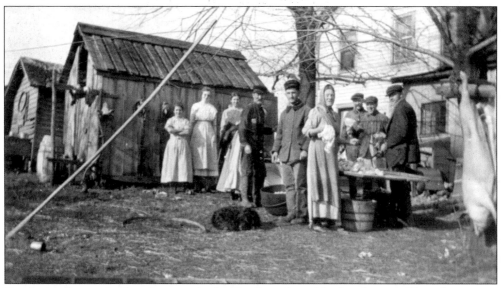

Butchering day on the farm becomes both a family and neighborhood event. These farmers are butchering hogs in Greene Township, c. 1917. (From the collection of the author.)

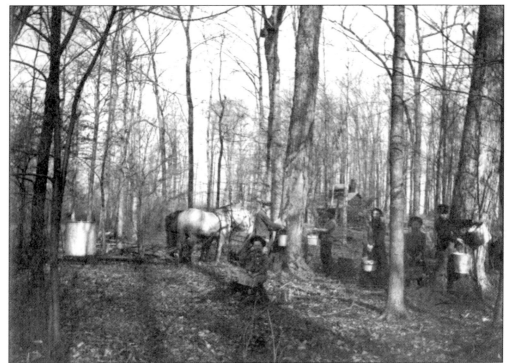

An indication that the long winter is nearing an end comes in February with the tapping of maple trees to gather sap for maple syrup. Several families around the Potato Creek area owned maple sugar camps. This photograph, c. 1900, shows members of the Cullar family tapping trees in Liberty Township. (From the collection of Joanne Carter.)

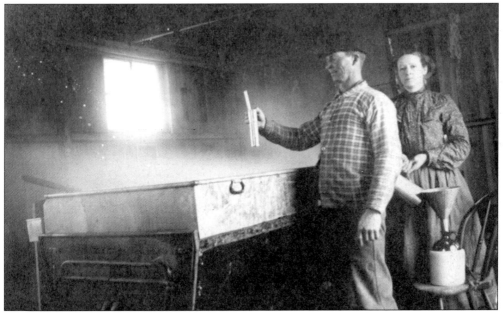

Mary Cullar observes as her husband William checks the thickness of his maple syrup c. 1900. (From the collection of Joanne Carter.)

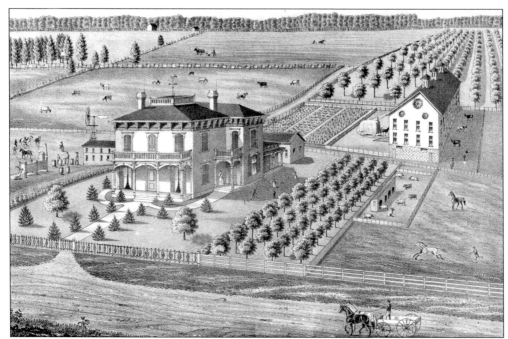

Adam Shidler was one of the area's best known pioneer farmers and saw mill owners. He was also a successful inventor. Mr. Shidler was the inventor of the float and stop device used in water closets, steam boilers, and in the gasoline supply of automobiles. He and his wife Mary (Klopfenstien) lived on this pristine farm in Union Township in 1875. (From the collection of the St. Joseph County Public Library.)

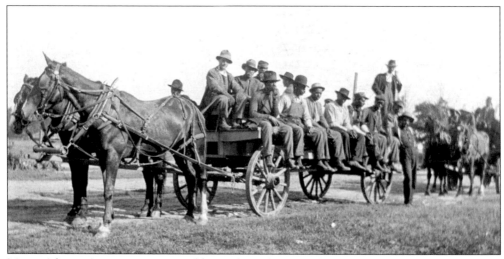

Many African-American men would travel via horse and wagon from South Bend to the farmlands outside of North Liberty to work in onion and mint fields. One such group poses on a wagon c. 1915. (From the collection of the author.)

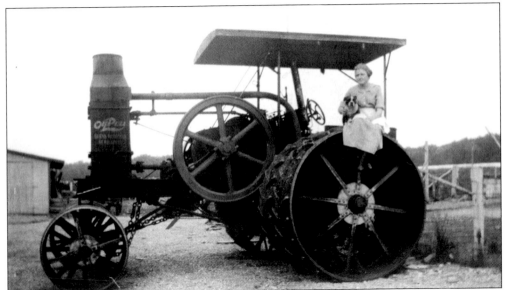

Today a relic, back then a marvel in modern technology! Ethel Turrell sits atop her family tractor in Greene Township c. 1917. (From the collection of the author.)

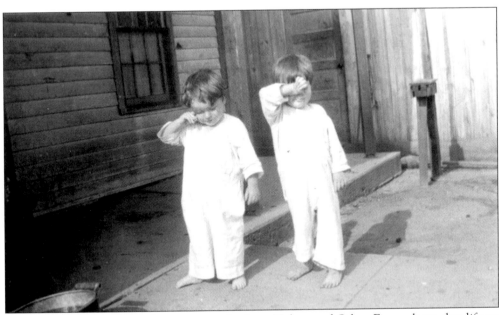

Wiping sun and sleep from their eyes, cousins Jerry Nelson and Orban Finney learn that life on the family farm starts bright and early. (From the collection of the author.)

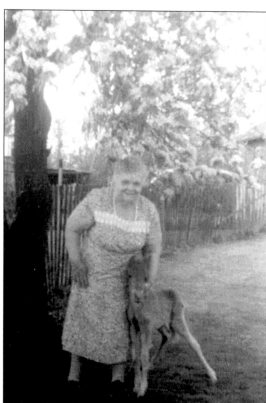

Only a few days old, the newborn colt "Seabiscuit" nuzzles up to Mabel Banks on a farm outside of North Liberty. (From the collection of the author.)

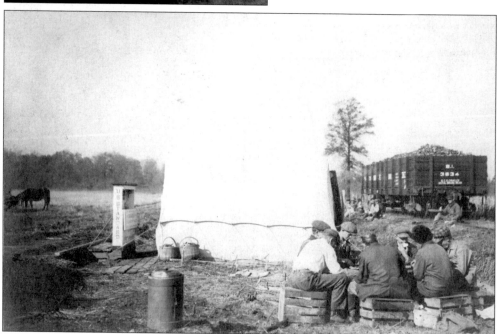

After filling several boxcars with turnips, these Greene Township farmers take a much-deserved break. The turnips were grown on the Fair Farm in the late 1910s, which today is owned by the Gumz family. (From the collection of the author.)

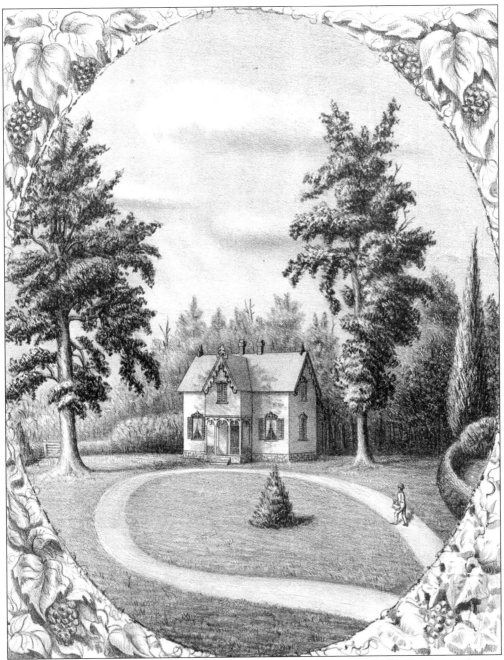

With over 500 apple trees, a pear orchard, an acre of grapes, and gardens filled with strawberries and vegetables, J.M. Swain of Greene Township had one of the most impressive fruit farms in the entire county. Mr. Swain's farm is depicted here in 1875. (From the collection of the St. Joseph County Public Library.)

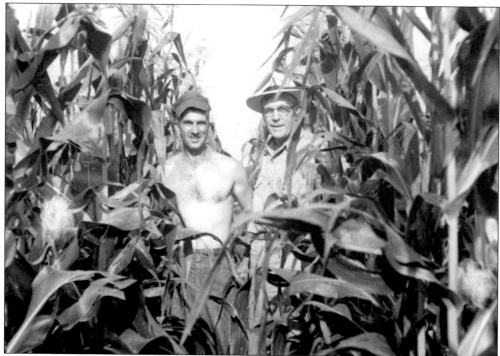

Herb Anderson proudly stands in his cornfield with a member of the county agriculture department on the Anderson farm located outside of North Liberty, c. 1950. (From the collection of Delores Anderson.)

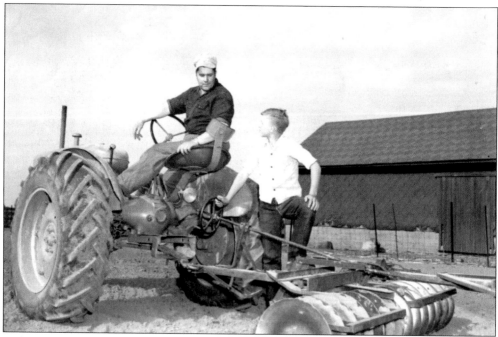

William Allsop of Greene Township takes a break from disking the family farm to chat with his son Richard in this spring of 1950. (From the collection of Judy Allsop.)

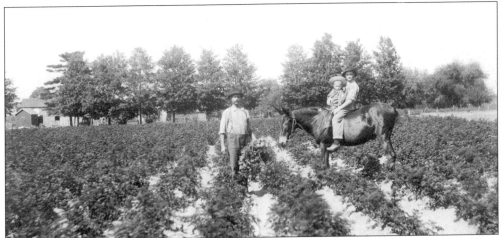

Potatoes have been a staple among residents in the county since first farmed by the Potawatomi Indians. It is believed the Potawatomis were the first to name Potato Creek as potatoes flourished in her banks. Shown in their Liberty Township potato field, from left to right, are: Alonzo Sheneman, Claude Sheneman and Dave Donathen c.1910. (From the collection of Gladys Sheneman.)

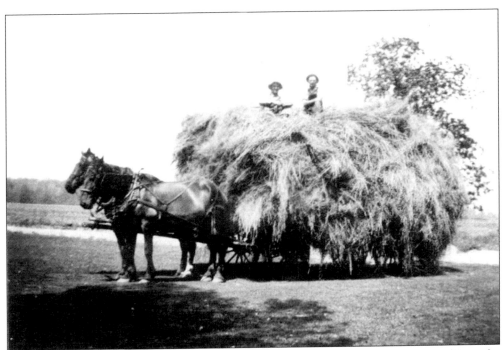

Two farmers from Lincoln Township sit atop a wagon overflowing with hay c. 1917. (From the collection of the Walter family.)

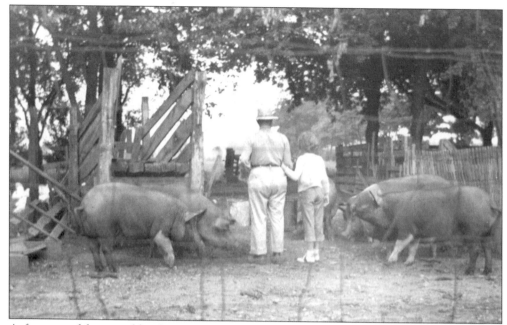

A farmer and his granddaughter stroll through a pigpen on this farm in Liberty Township. (From the collection of the author.)

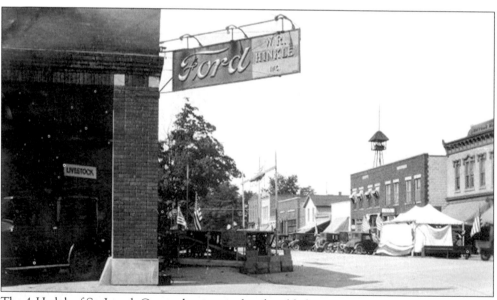

The 4-H club of St. Joseph County has inspired and molded youngsters interested in agriculture and home economics for over 75 years. The fair, pictured here c. 1935, was held for several years in North Liberty. For the next ten years it was held in the town of Lakeville. (From the collection of the St. Joseph County 4-H Fair.)

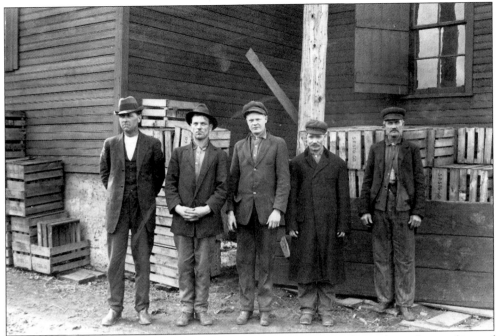

This group of men stands outside the Piowatty Onion Storage located on the outskirts of Walkerton c. 1915. (From the collection of the Walkerton Area Historical Society.)

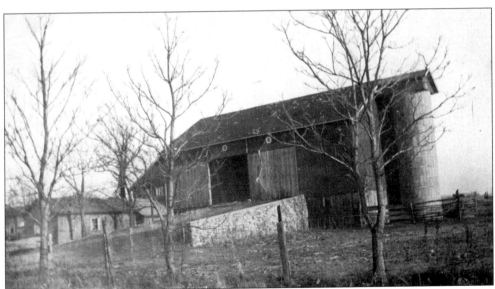

Like many area barns built in the 1800s, the base of this barn in Liberty Township was built from stones gathered from nearby fields. Sadly, time and weather have taken their toll and few of these impressive barns remain. (From the collection of Delores Anderson.)

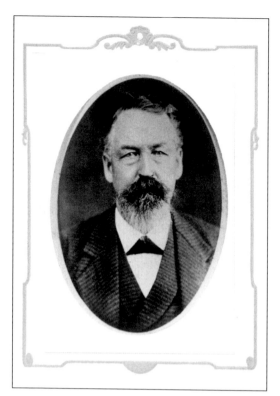

During the time of the Civil War, many local farmers were drafted into duty. If one had enough money they could pay to have a replacement sent instead. However, N.J. Turrell of Union Township would not hear of it. When drafted he refused to have a substitute saying he could hire no better man than he to fill his place. (From the collection of the author.)

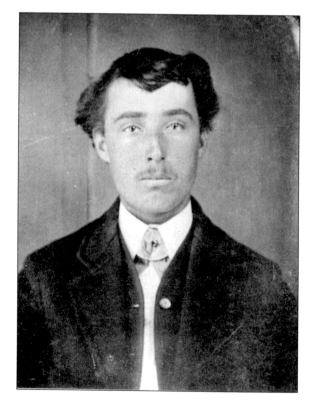

George Sylvester Hill of Greene Township was also called to duty for the Union Army. Mr. Hill was a 2nd Lieutenant in the 8th U.S. Heavy Artillery. (From the collection of the late Ruth Finch.)

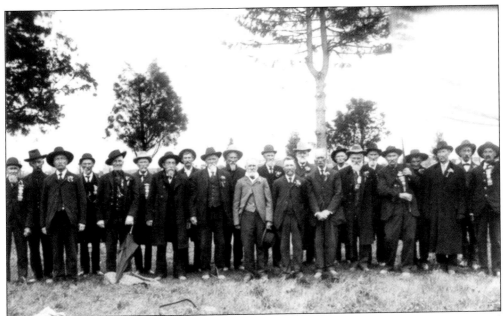

The Grand Army of the Republic was an organization comprised of Union veterans of the Civil War. Pictured here are members of the Jesse Coppock Chapter of the GAR. Coppock, a native of the Walketon area, was a corporal in Company D of the 54th Infantry and died in the line of duty. This chapter, named in memory of Coppock, met in and around Walkerton from 1884 to1923. (From the collection of the Walkerton Area Historical Society.)

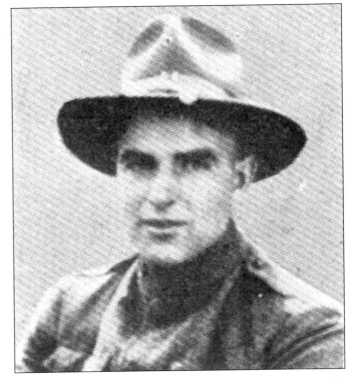

Edward Zurcher Sousley, a farmhand from North Liberty, was one of several young men called to fight during World War I. On July 20, 1918 during the battle of Soissons, Mr. Sousley was killed in action. He is buried in the American Cemetery in Aisne, France. (From the Collection of the St. Joseph County Public Library.)

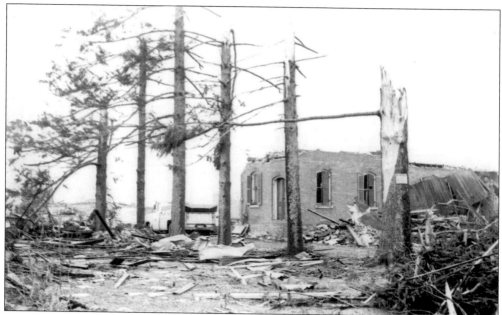

The worst disaster to hit Southern St. Joseph County came on the evening of April 11, 1965, Palm Sunday. Around 6 p.m. an intense storm front moved in and tornadoes roared their way through Union and Madison Townships. Many homes, such as Anna Schalliol's of Madison Township, pictured here, were severely damaged or destroyed. (From the collection of the Mishawaka-Penn-Harris Public Library.)

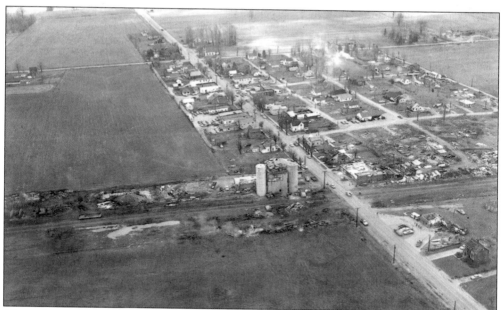

More than one-third of the community of Wyatt was destroyed from the Palm Sunday Tornadoes, as seen here in this aerial view. As widespread as the damage was there, thankfully no one lost their lives in Madison Township. Four people were killed in Lakeville; statewide 137 people lost their lives on that day. (From the collection of the Mishawaka-Penn-Harris Public Library.)

Three

SCHOOL DAYS

*"I have had playmates, I have had companions,
In my days of childhood, in my joyful school days–
All, all are gone, the old familiar faces."*

–Charles Lamb

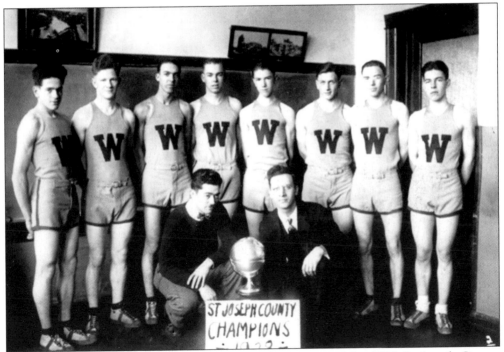

These boys from Walkerton High School were the winners of the 1928 St. Joseph County Basketball Championship. Pictured, from left to right, are: (front row) Coach D.C. Chezem and Principal E.J. Hippenstelle; (back row) Myron Mullett, Ray Nusbaum, Clarence Shultz, Wayne Cover, Roy Sheaks, Arthur DeMyer, and Louis Houser. (From the collection of the Walkerton Area Historical Society.)

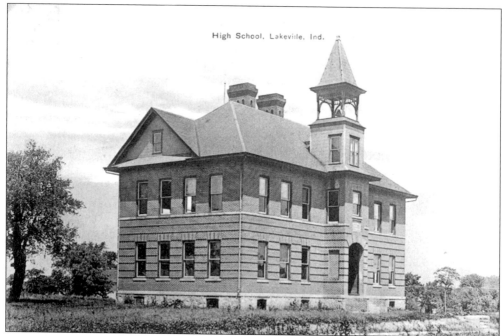

High School, Lakeville, Ind.

In 1898, the first high school in Lakeville was built on Main and Harrison Streets, pictured here c. 1915. In 1931, a new high school was built and this building became the grade school. The building was torn down in 1969. (From the collection of Toni Cook.)

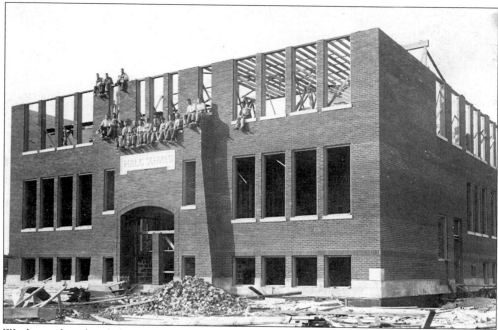

Workers take a break from construction of the Walkerton High School in 1914. This building remained the town's high school until a more modern one was built in 1942. (From the collection of the Walkerton Area Historical Society.)

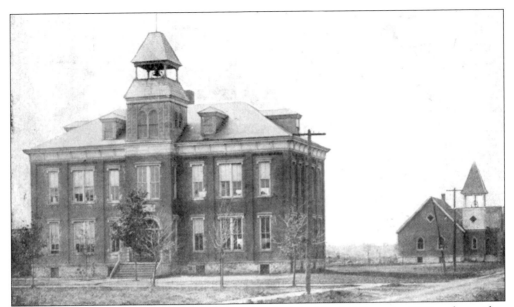

This schoolhouse, pictured here c. 1915, was first built in North Liberty in 1892 and served as the grammar school. By the fall of 1898 it was being used as the high school. It remained the town's high school until a new building was built north of town in 1926. The North Liberty First Brethren Church is seen in the background. (From the collection of Toni Cook.)

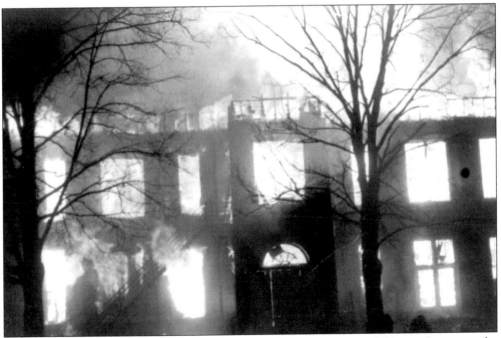

While no longer used as a school since 1926, but rather by the Matz Implement Company, the old school house burned down in a spectacular blaze on February 23, 1956. Besides the North Liberty Fire Department, the towns of Walkerton, Lakeville, and LaPaz sent their departments to battle the intense blaze. (From the collection of the town of North Liberty.)

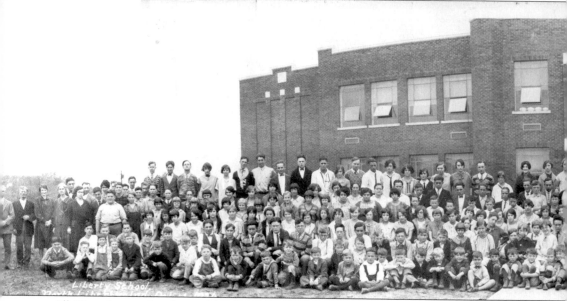

All 12 grades stand in front of the new North Liberty school house which opened in the fall of 1926. After a more modern high school was built in 1956, this building was used as the grade school. After the merger of North Liberty High School and John Glenn High School in 1982, the

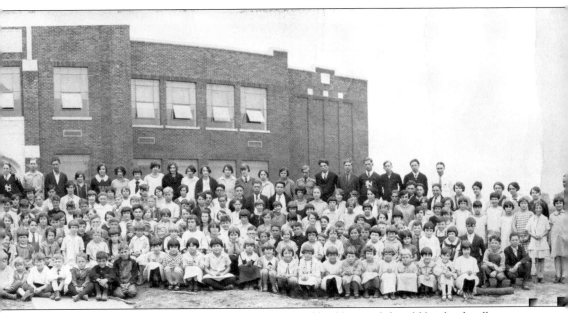

elementary school was moved into the former high school building and the old brick schoolhouse succumbed to the wrecking ball. (From the collection of North Liberty Elementary School.)

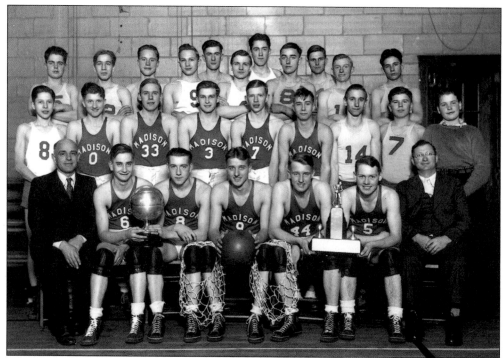

In 1936, the Madison High School boy's basketball team won the county championship. Rudy Marker, bottom row far left, and Alva Marburger, bottom row far right, coached them to victory. (From the collection of the Mishawaka-Penn-Harris Public Library.)

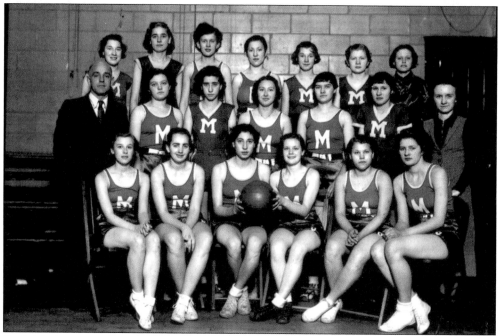

Rudy Marker, second row far left, also coached the 1936 Madison High School girls' basketball team. (From the collection of the Mishawaka-Penn-Harris Public Library.)

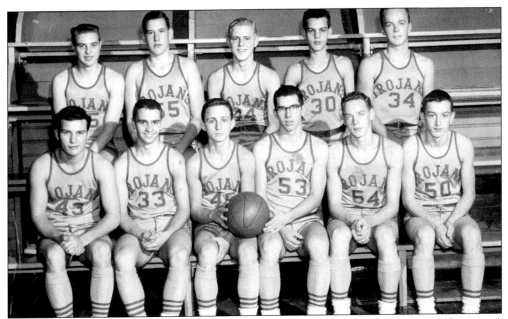

Members of the 1957 Lakeville "B" Team, pictured here from left to right, are: (front row) Harley Schafer, Joe Carrico, Roger Schafer, Wayne Weiss, Don Hall, Rolland Miller; (back row) Charles Konkle, Larry Ort, Lewis Hayes, Richard Jordan, and Keith Lineback. (From the collection of the St. Joseph County Public Library.)

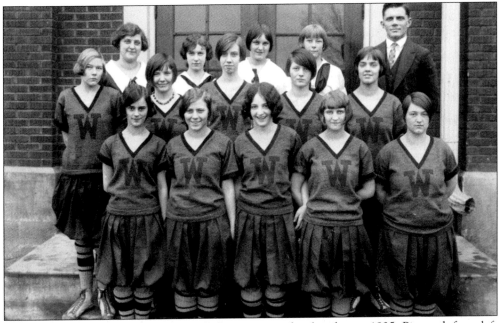

Walkerton High School's girls' basketball team poses for this shot c. 1935. Pictured, from left to right, are: (front row) Hortense Shirley, Opal Lawrence, Rosamond Nusbaum, Myrtle Johnson, Jane Griffin; (second row) Wilma Casey, Marjorie Holser, Irma Winner, Margaret Griffin, Inez Truax; (back row) Coach Coy, Edna Steele, Doris Bierly, Bertha Ward, and Coach McLaughlin. (From the collection of the Walkerton Area Historical Society.)

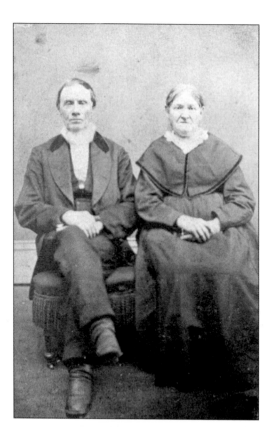

Like many pioneer farmers, Washington Hummer donated a portion of his land so that a one-room schoolhouse could be built. For their generosity the school was often named for the families who donated their land. Pictured here are Mr. Hummer and his wife Mercy (Garwood) Hummer in the 1870s. (From the collection of the author.)

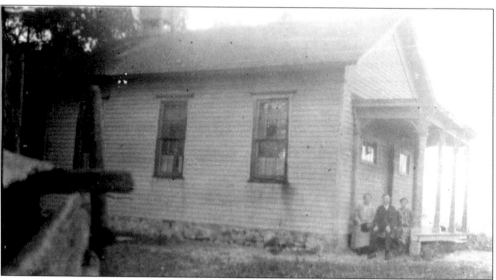

The Hummer Schoolhouse stood on the corner of Madison and Mulberry Roads in Greene Township from the 1870s to the 1930s. It is pictured here c. 1917. (From the collection of the author.)

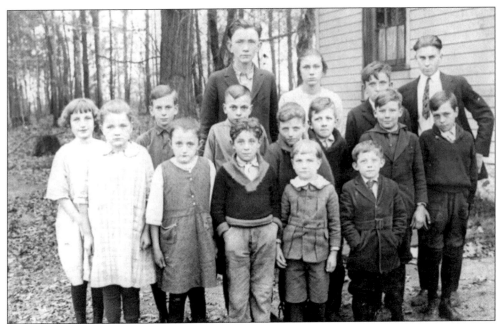

Pupils of the one-room Hummer Schoolhouse pictured here in 1922, from left to right, are: (front row) Mildred Kane, Lela Kane, John Kierein, Carl Gombor, William Kierein; (second row) Irene Gombor, Cleon Kettering, Ralph Seward, John Deitsch, Arthur Hummer, Wayne Clemens, George Hummer, (back row) Chester Kane, Frances Kane, Ralph Kane, and the teacher Everett Hartsall. (From the collection of Mary Kierein.)

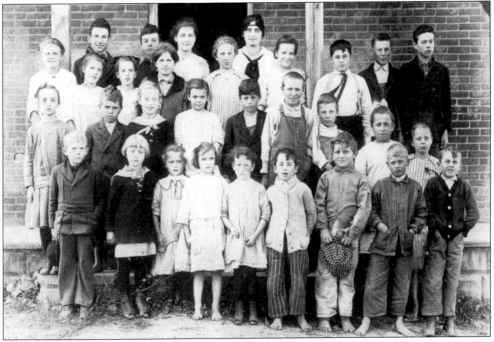

Seen here, c. 1915, are the students of the Stringtown Schoolhouse located on the corners of St. Road 4 and Redwood Road. (From the collection of Gladys Sheneman.)

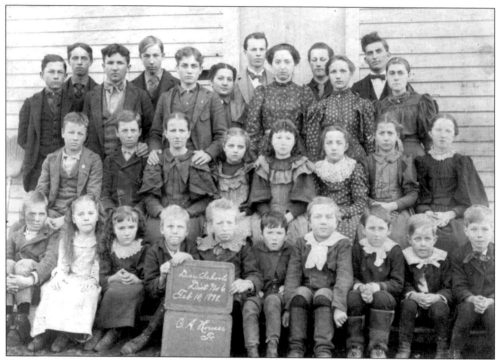

Students of the one-room Dice School, in Liberty Township, pose for their class picture in 1898. Standing in the back row, to the far right, is schoolteacher C.A. Houser. (From the collection of Gladys Albright.)

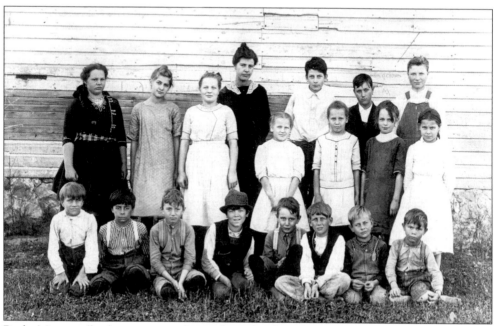

Ruth Mangus (back row, center) stands with all eight grades of the one-room Bickel Schoolhouse located on Liberty Trail in Liberty Township c. 1915. (From the collection of Joanne Carter.)

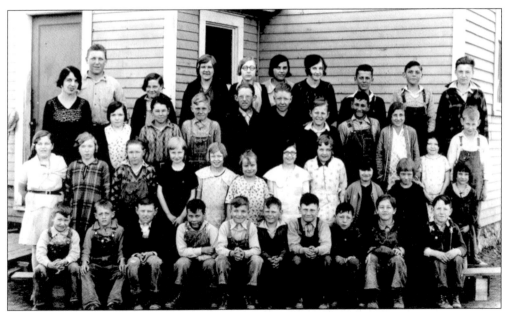

Students of the Slough Schoolhouse in Union Township are seen here c. 1930. (From the collection of Eileen Copsey.)

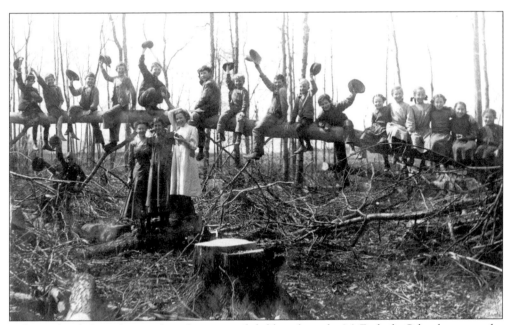

Taking a break from their studies, this group of children from the McEndarfer School wave to the camera. Located on the corner of Oak and Riley Roads in Liberty Township, the school was taught by Sofia Albright when this picture was taken c. 1910. (From the collection of Joanne Carter.)

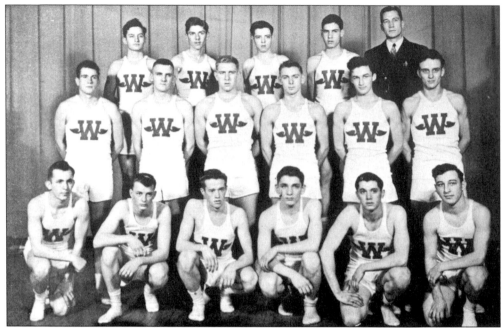

The 1947 Walkerton Indian's track team poses for this group shot, c. 1947. Pictured, from left to right, are: (front row) John Guttman, Roger Savage, Dick Northam, Bob Urbin, Ora Harder, Charles Rugers; (second row) Charles Harness, Charles Decker, Art LaBere, Don Arseneau, DeWayne Pavey, Bob Smith; (back row) Kevin Huffstetter, Charles DuVall, Glenn Kaser, Donnell Cogswell, and Coach Smalley. (From the collection of Norma Schmeltz.)

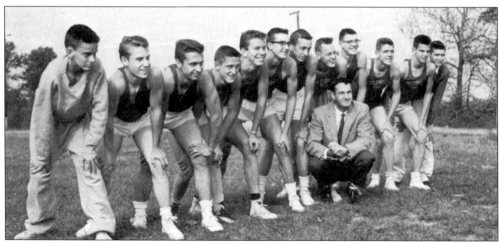

The 1959 Lakeville Trojans cross country team, pictured from left to right, are: E. Jordan, R. Annis, J. Carrico, M. Pilger, P. Stradley, J. Fuchs, R. Miller, D. Hall, R. Riddle, G. Modlin, Manager T. Wallis, Manager and Coach J. Ellers. (From the collection of the St. Joseph County Public Library.)

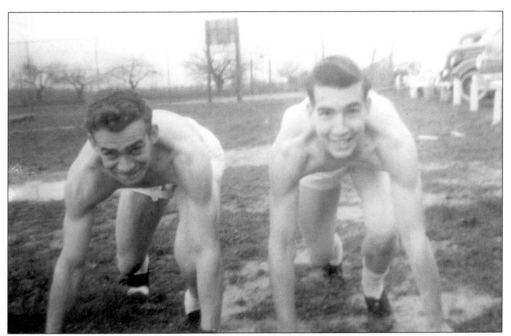

Dale Gouker and Jim Houser perfect their starting stance for the North Liberty High School track team in 1950. (From the collection of Pat Mortakis.)

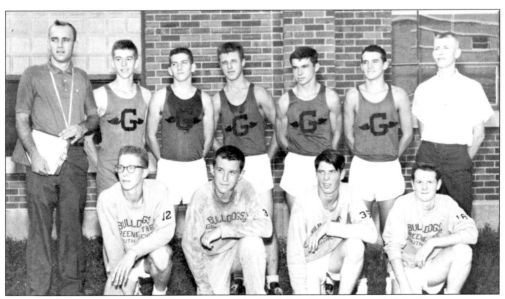

After an intense afternoon of running, members of the 1962 Greene Bulldog's cross country team pose for this team shot. (From the collection of the St. Joseph County Public Library.)

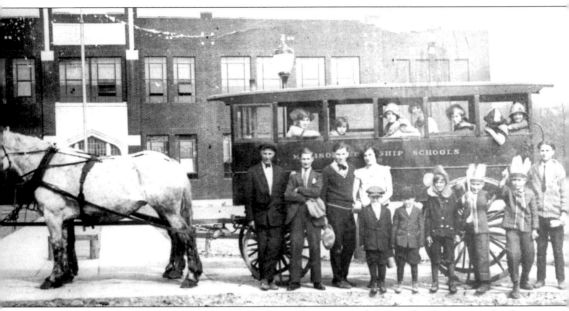

Madison Township's first transportation for students to and from school was via this horse drawn bus *c.* 1920. The bus is parked in front of the Madison School. (From the collection of Peggy Marker.)

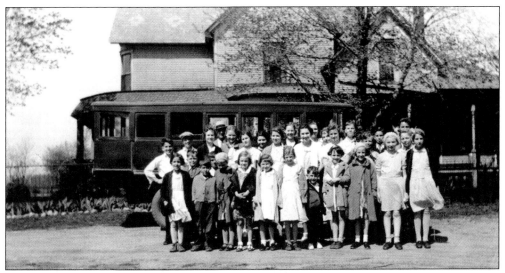

Bus driver George Anderson, back row with the hat, stands with a group of his passengers, *c.* 1935. Bus driving became a family tradition as two of his sons, Herb and Paul, also became bus drivers for the North Liberty Schools. (From the collection of Paul Anderson.)

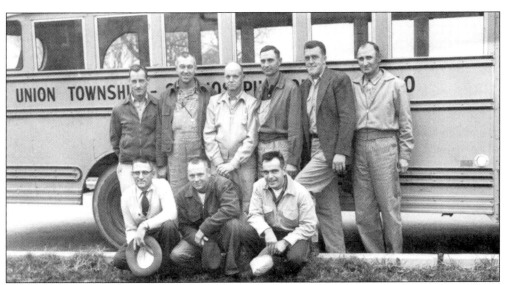

The 1958 bus drivers for the Union Township School's, from left to right, are: (front row) Art Showalter, Russell Geyer, Glen Plummer; (back row) Dwight Eslinger, Woodrow Riddle, Merl Haskins, Walter Shutz, Pete, Frick and Aaron Rouch. (From the collection of the St. Joseph County Public Library.)

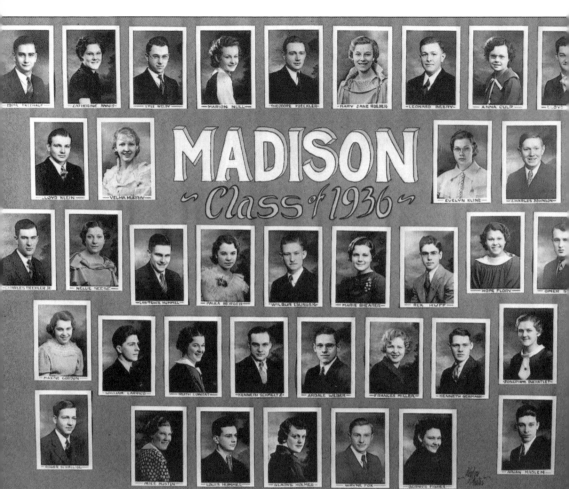

Members of the 1936 Madison High School class of 1936, from left to right, are: (front row) Roger Schalliol, Alice Austin, Louis Hummel, Gladys Holms, Wayne Fox, Bernice Fisher, Arvan Maolem; (second row) Maxine Gordon, William Carrico, Ruth Contat, Kenneth Schmeltz, Ardale Weber, Frances Miller, Kenneth Germann, Josephine Duchatlet ; (third row) Charles Beehler Jr., Nellie Seese, Lawrence Hummel, Paula Berger, Wilbur Eslinger, Marie Shearer, Rex Huff, Hope Flory, Omer Seese; (fourth row) Lloyd Klein, Velma Murphy, Evelyn Kline, Charles Johnson; (back row) Edgar Freehauf, Catherine Annis, Lyle Weldy, Marion Null, Theodore Foeckler, Mary Jane Roeder, Leonard Beery, Anna Culp, and Lloyd Berrey. (From the collection of the Mishawaka-Penn-Harris Public Library.)

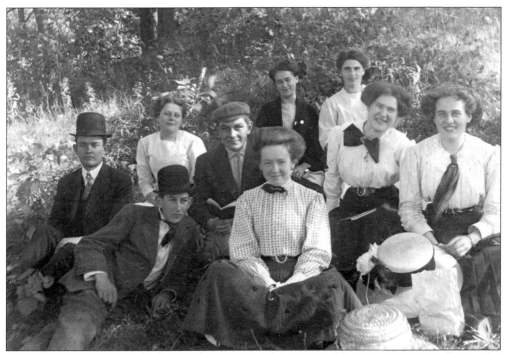

The Walkerton High School class of 1911 relaxes in a field outside of town. (From the collection of the Walkerton Area Historical Society.)

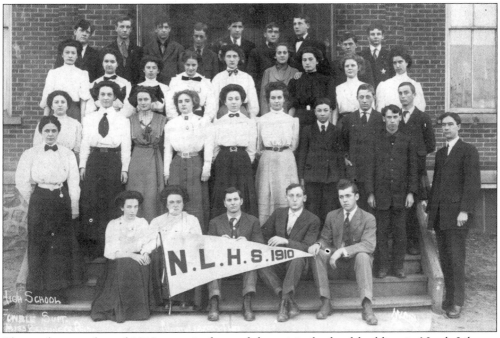

The graduating class of 1910 poses in front of the original school building in North Liberty. (From the collection of Joanne Carter.)

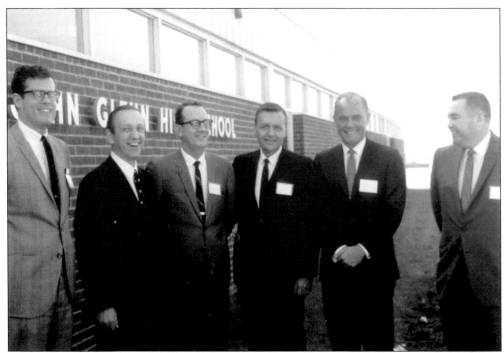

Astronaut John Glenn, second from the left, stands with school board members at the dedication of the new John Glenn High School on October 20, 1968. (From the collection of the Walkerton Area Historical Society.)

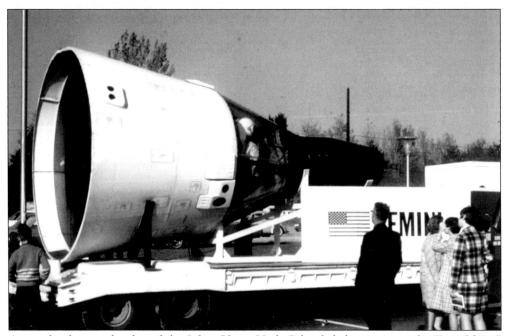

A popular feature the day of the John Glenn High School dedication was the Friendship 7 Mercury capsule in which John Glenn became the first man to orbit the earth on February 20, 1962. (From the collection of the Walkerton Area Historical Society.)

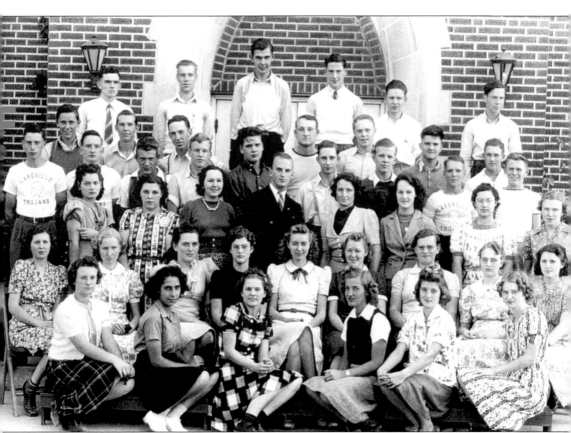

Members of the Lakeville High School class of 1940. Pictured, from left to right, are: (front row) Helen Huff, Winifred Shupert, Betty Barkley, Martha Plummer, Virginia Sheets, Hildegarde Beasics; (second row) Marian Schrader, Eileen Kline, Adeline Marek, Mary Garrett, Virginia Berry, Betty Berry, Hazel Bennett, Harriet Hildebrand, Marjorie Plummer; (third row) Margaret Miers, Marjorie Schafer, Glee Herbster, Mr. Harold Waddell and Ms. Marvoline Hostetler, Ruth Welsh, Marguerite Rouch, Dorothy Cunlain; (fourth Row) Lyle Schafer, Leland Donathen, Bob LaCrone, John Barkley, Henry Getz, Jack Miller, John Long, Harold Geyer, Herbert Kelley; (fifth row) Joseph Konkle, Herbert Swathwood, Rulo Conrad, Ross Fuchs, Marley Arthurholtz, Paul Nicholas, Howard Siefer; (sixth row) Elwin McLouth, Bennoie Rice, Eugene Watkins, Dorlen Murphy, Kenneth Burroughs, and Eugene Sanders. (From the collection of Eileen Copsey.)

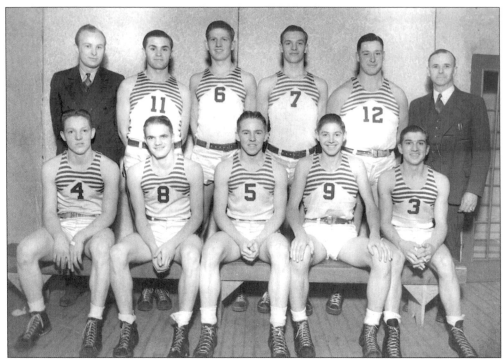

The North Liberty Shamrocks basketball team of 1941 pictured from, left to right, (front row) Neil Jackson, Don Hay, Joe Jackson, Joe Dalke, Herb Anderson; (back row) Coach Jim Jenkins, Bill Day, Carl Folk, Junior Heim, Duwaine Liggett, and Principal J.W. Gentry. (From the collection of Delores Anderson.)

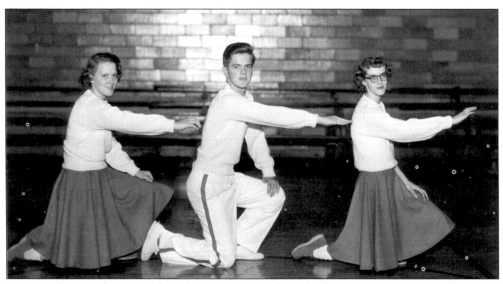

Keeping the crowd interested in the game, even when the home team is down, falls on the shoulders of the cheer team. Members of the 1950 North Liberty High School cheer team are, from left to right, Joyce Peddycord, Jack Kos, and Frances Hammaker. (From the collection of Pat Farrar.)

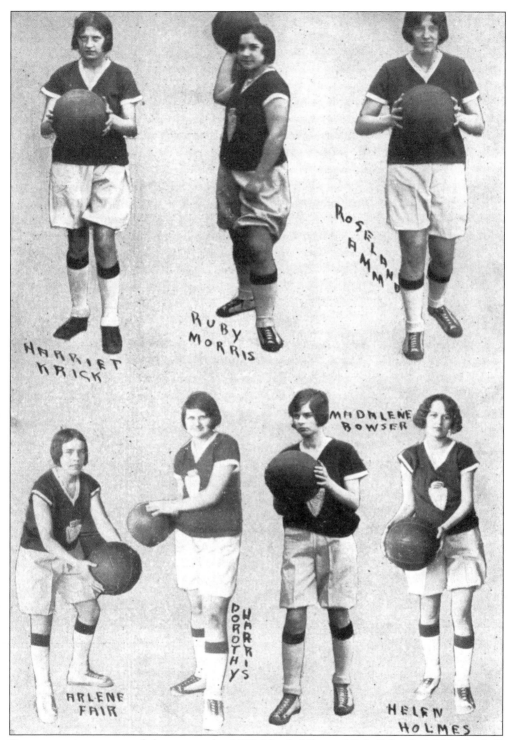

Demonstrating moves of the game, the 1929 North Liberty High School girls' basketball team shows that the boys aren't the only ones who can handle a ball. (From the collection of Gladys Albright.)

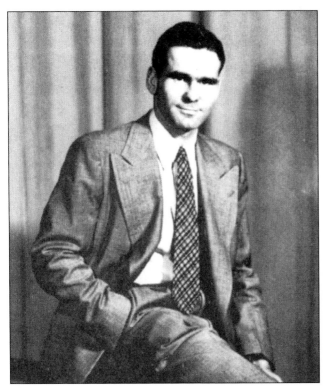

Coaches instill confidence and the rules of the game onto their young players. Don Bunge, who went on to great success in nearby Bremen, got his start as both a teacher and coach for Walkerton High School. Coach Bunge is seen here in 1950. (From the collection of the Walkerton-Lincoln Township Public Library.)

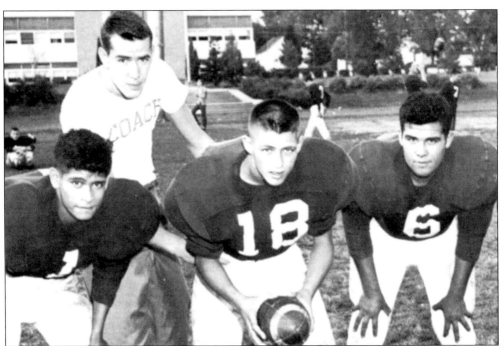

Members of the 1960 Walkerton High School football team take a break from practice to pose for this photo. They are, Coach Jim Warren, Jacob Barron, Ernie Morrison, and Joe Arce. (From the collection of the Walkerton-Lincoln Township Public Library.)

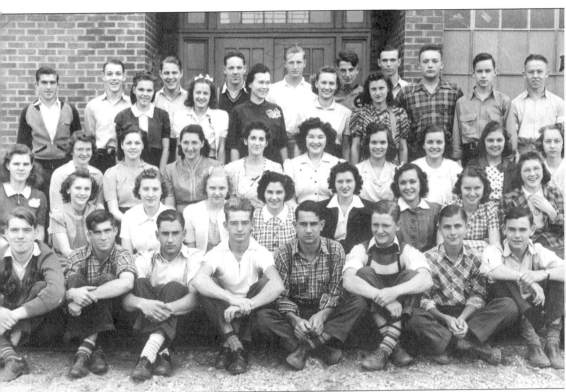

Members of North Liberty High School's class of 1942 pose for their junior year picture. Pictured, from left to right, are: (front row) Franklin Sousley, Howard Arnold, Vincent Imbroguglio, Robert Rowles, Harold Clark, Ralph Nelson, Ralph Hartsough, Emery Thomas; (second row) Beatrice Lick, Esther Collins, Helen Newcomer, Ruth Bowers, Phyllis Boles, Florence Dalk, Betty Fair, Myrna Williams, Doris Fritz; (third row) Betty Sheneman, Betty Reed, Byrdie Driebelbis. Mary Alward, Evelyn Kime, Marietta Rodgers, Ruby Whitinger, Irene Gouker, Gloria Rupe; (fourth row) Martha Ames, Florence Nelson, Miss. Robertson, Lucille Waco, Julia Molnar; (back row) Herbert Anderson, Branson Hiatt, Dale Knepp, Neal Jackson, Robert Shupert, Robert Klinedinst, William Heim, James Wesolek, Robert Shafer, and Joseph Jackson. (From the collection of the author.)

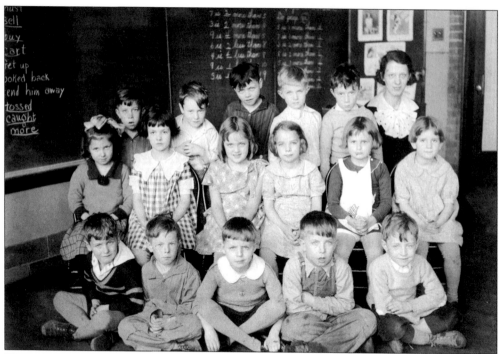

This 1930 North Liberty first grade class was taught by Miss Roseland Amm. (From the collection of Fauntelle Spellman.)

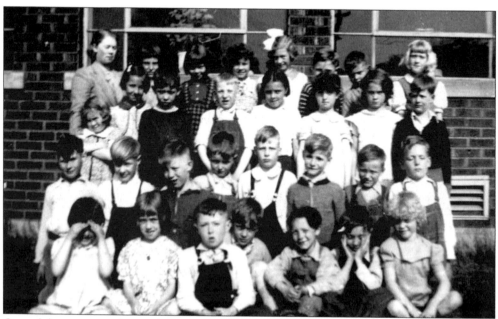

One of the most popular teachers in all of Liberty Township was Faye Mangus. Mrs. Mangus, who was Miss Steele at the time, stands with one of her first classes in 1938. (From the collection of Faye Steele Mangus.)

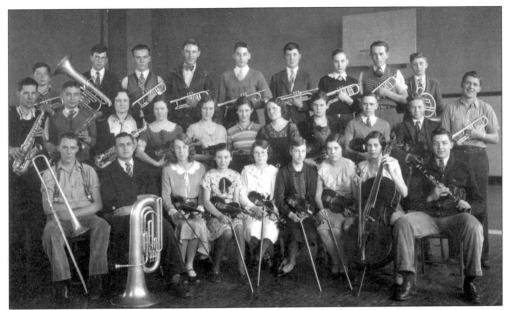

Proudly posing with their musical instruments are members of the Walkerton High School Band *c.* 1935. (From the collection of the Walkerton Area Historical Society.)

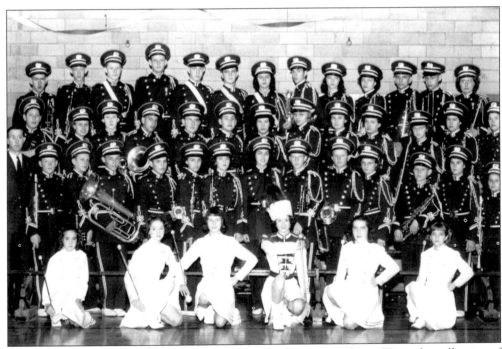

The 1953 North Liberty High School Marching Band is pictured here. (From the collection of Donn McDaniel.)

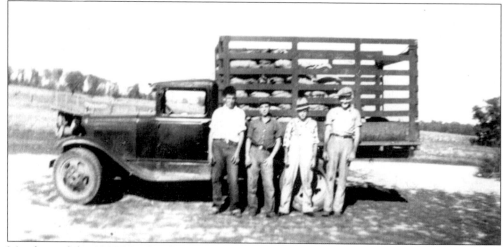

Members of the 1939 North Liberty High School F.F.A (Future Farmers of America) proudly stand in front of the 82 bushels of potatoes they dug. Pictured, from left to right, are: Joe Imbro, Lloyd Kaser, Paul Shoemaker, and Dale Nelson. (From the collection of the author.)

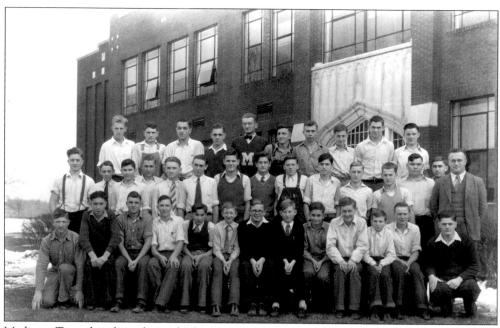

Madison Township has always had a strong farming community. The Future Farmers of America club at Madison High School helped ensure this tradition would continue. Members of the 1931 F.F.A. are seen here in front of the school. (From the collection of Peggy Marker.)

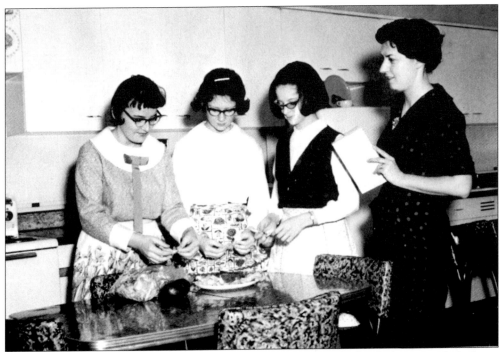

Home Economics taught young women the finer points of foods, family living, and clothing. Pictured in the North Liberty High School Home Economics Department, from left to right, are: Kay Simms, Grace Scott, Susan Wentz, and teacher Melba Holmgren. (From the collection of the St. Joseph County Public Library.)

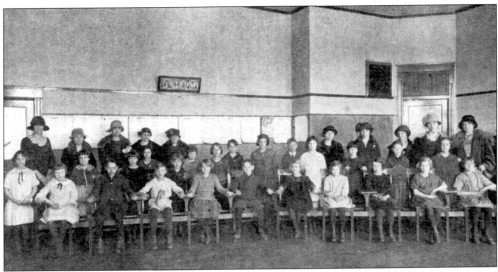

Proud mothers stand behind their healthy children in the North Liberty Health and Nutrition class in 1924. (From the collection of the St. Joseph County Public Library.)

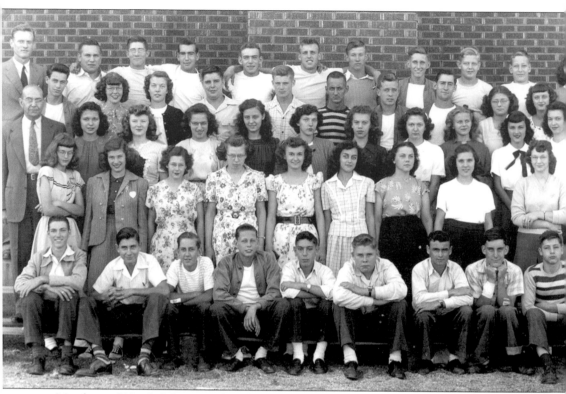

Members of North Liberty High School's class of 1950 pose for their sophomore year class photo. Pictured here, from left to right, are: (front row) Rolland Fitz, Paul Goon, Bruce Dixon, Eugene Singelton, James Ansbaugh, Carl Bostwick, Robert Huling, Clarence Cooper, Ted Lewis; (second row) Frances Hammaker, Louis Mapes, Joan Devine, Alice Kane, Veleda Newland, Elsie Rowe, Elearnor Irvine, Enid Walsh, Clarice Kime; (third row) Mr. Agness, Pat Farrar, Sandra Carroll, Mina Jarvis, Louetta Peddycord, Evelyn Platyts, Juanita Six, Kay Brown, Susie Fair, (fourth row) Dick Reed, Normalee Housholder, Connie Kizer, Jack Warner, Worth Johnson, Junior Ford, Frank Rauen, Don Clark, Lucille Liggett, Judy Fair; (back row) Mr. Leasure, Clyde Newcome, Gene Springman, Jim Houser, Dale Gouker, George Becktol, Harold Hansen, Roy Clark, Jerry Peterson, Wayne Wilcox, and Delores Lightfoot. (From the collection of Pat Mortakis.)

Four
BUSINESS

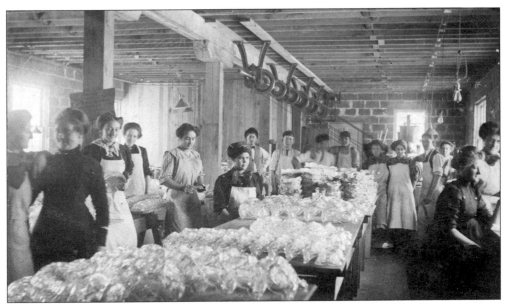

Making everything from glass sugar bowls to creamers, the Central Cut Glass Factory opened in Walkerton in 1910. The factory thrived for nearly a decade until fire destroyed it in 1919. It was never rebuilt. Workers are shown in the factory c. 1915. (From the collection of the Walkerton Area Historical Society.)

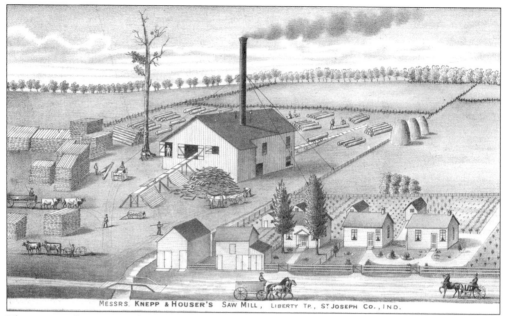

MESSRS. **KNEPP & HOUSER'S** SAW MILL, LIBERTY TP., ST JOSEPH CO., IND.

There is no finer example of the phrase, "If at first you don't succeed..." than that of Levi Knepp. Owner and operating of the Knepp and Houser Saw Mill in Liberty Township, Mr. Knepp rebuilt the business twice after fire destroyed it shortly after he bought it in 1865 and again around 1869. The saw mill is show here in 1875. (From the Collection of the St. Joseph County Public Library.)

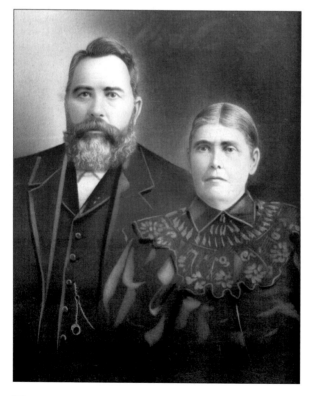

The owner and operator of the Knepp and Houser saw mill, Levi Knepp with his wife Sarah Houser Knepp, is seen here. (From the collection of Gladys (Knepp) Albright.)

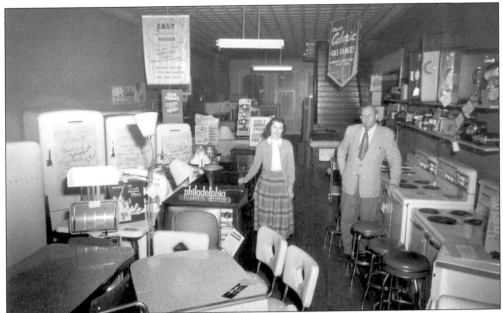

Faunt S. LeRoy was well known throughout the entire county for his furniture and appliance stores in both Walkerton and North Liberty. In business for over 40 years, Mr. LeRoy always offered the finest up-to-date merchandise at a reasonable price. He is seen here with one of his employees in the mid 1950s. (From the collection or Eric Nelson.)

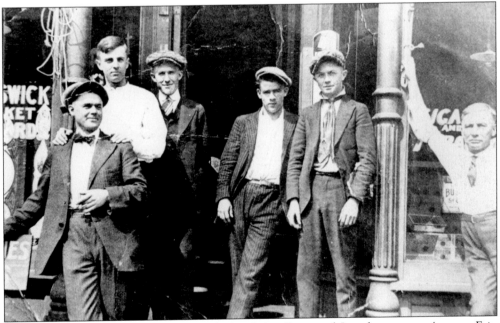

This group of men leisurely stands in front of the Cigar and Lunch store on Avenue F in Walkerton. Curry Miller owned the store for many years before he sold it and it became the popular Shirley's Restaurant. Pictured, from left to right, are: unidentified, Dallas Miller unidentified, Stub Northam, Gust Kerchaert, and unidentified. (From the collection of the Walkerton Area Historical Society.)

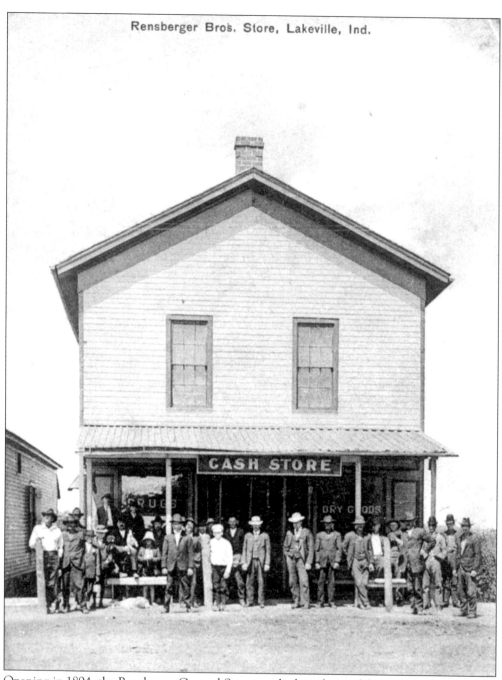

Opening in 1894, the Rensberger General Store supplied residents of the town with everything from dry goods to boots and jewelry. Lester and Clarence Rensberger owned the store. This postcard, dated the first week of February 1915, was used as an advertisement for the store. Specials that week included: 100 pounds of sugar for $5.40, coffee for 14¢ a pound, backing powder 22¢, and ten pounds of peaches 95¢ a pound! (From the collection of Toni Cook.)

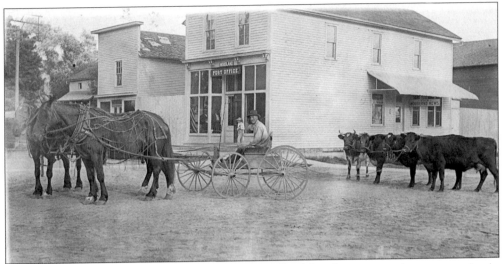

While not officially an incorporated town, Woodland has been an active community in Madison Township since 1860. This photo shows Woodland as it appeared in 1900 with a population of about 90 people. The Woodland Post Office and the Woodland News can be seen in the background. (From the collection of Toni Cook.)

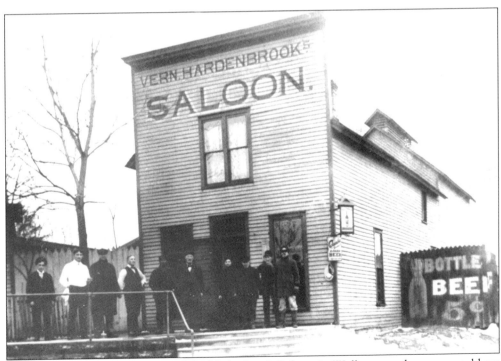

A group of men gather in front of the Hadenbrook Saloon in Walkerton, where you could get a bottle of beer for 5¢ a bottle! (From the collection of the Walkerton Area Historical Society.)

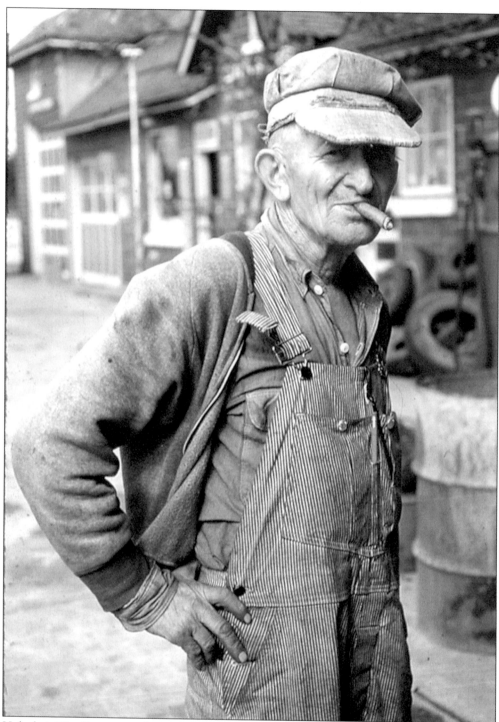

Huhnke's Tire Service was located over the railroad tracks in Walkerton on St. Road 23. This father and son business was opened by Albert A. Huhnke Sr. in the 1930s. It is seen here *c*. 1955. Later operated by Albert Jr., the station remained open until his death in the late 1990s. (From the collection of the Walkerton Area Historical Society.)

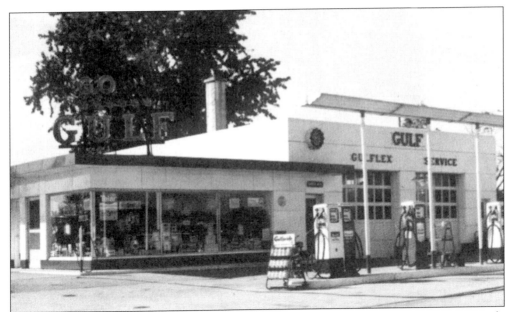

The Rupe Filling Station, located on the corners of Mayflower and State Road 23 was not only one of the only businesses in all of Greene Township, but the only place to get gas between North Liberty and South Bend! The station is seen here in 1962. (From the collection of the St. Joseph County Public Library.)

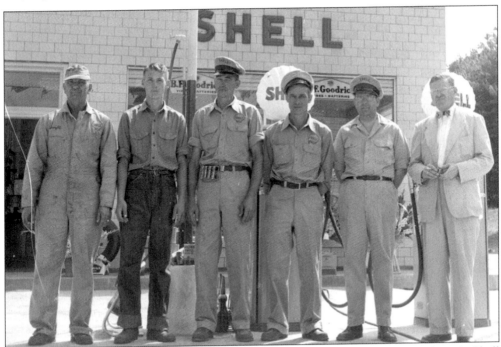

Located on the corners of U.S.31 and Harrison Street in Lakeville, Dwight Eslinger's Shell Station saw its grand opening in August of 1950. Pictured here in front of the station, from left to right, are: Windel Pugh, Duane Eslinger, Raymond Riddle, Mr. Eslinger, (unknown) and Harry Spires. (From the collection of Duane Eslinger.)

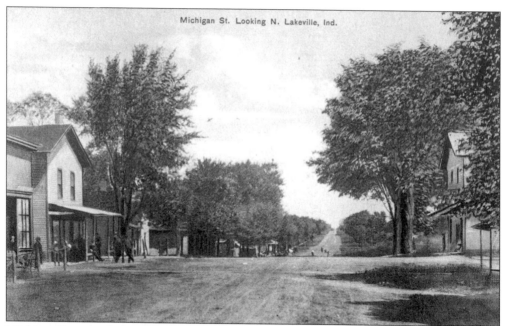

Michigan Street in Lakeville is seen in this *c.* 1915 photograph at a time when it was no more than a dirt road connecting the town to South Bend. Today, thousands of cars pass daily on Michigan Street, more commonly known as U.S. 31, linking South Bend to Indianapolis. (From the collection of Toni Cook.)

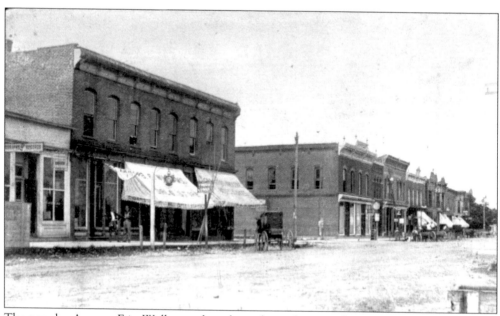

The popular Avenue F in Walkerton has always been the main business distract in the town. Today, Avenue F is more commonly known as U.S. 6.and Roosevelt Road. In 1953, it was designated as the "Grand Army of the Republic Highway" in honor of Union veterans of the Civil War. (From the collection of Toni Cook.)

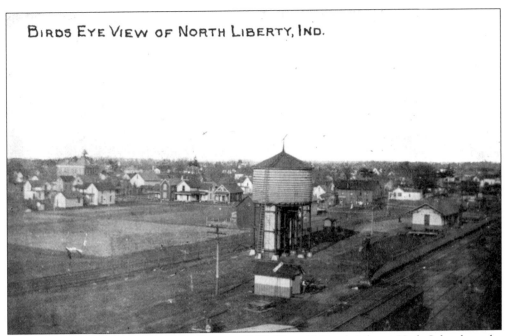

BIRDS EYE VIEW OF NORTH LIBERTY, IND.

This is a bird's-eye-view of North Liberty c. 1910. The old North Liberty High School can be seen in the upper left hand side of the horizon. Today, the Dollar General Store stands where the school once stood. (From the collection of Toni Cook.)

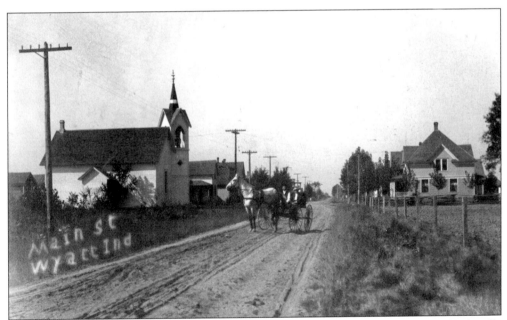

Located on the old Wabash Railroad Line, the community of Wyatt is located east of Lakeville in Madison Township. The town was platted in 1894 by Jeremiah Bechtel and is seen here c. 1917. (From the collection of Toni Cook.)

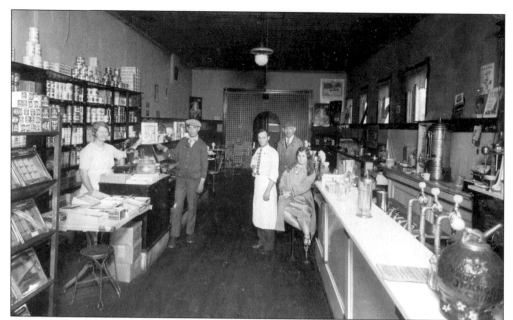

Gordon's Store, run by Tom Gordon, was located at 600 Roosevelt Road in Walkerton. Mr. Gordon is seen in the center of his store with the apron, his wife stands behind the counter to the left. (From the collection of the Walkerton Area Historical Society.)

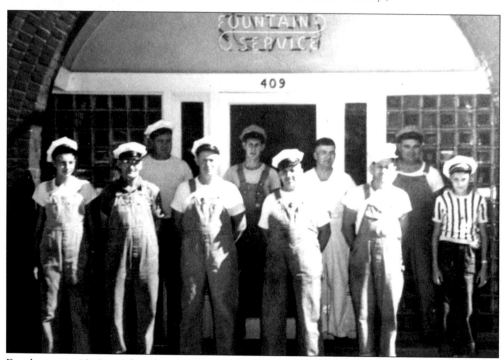

Employees in 1949 stand at the entrance of the Dairy Bar located in Walkerton. Pictured, from left to right, are: (front row) Tome Frame, Fritz Skinner, Dave Lawrence, Sam Frame, Raymond Beagles, and John Garab Jr.; (back row) Art Corner, (?) Holderread, Clarence Eichhorst, and Ernie Corner. (From the collection of the Walkerton Area Historical Society.)

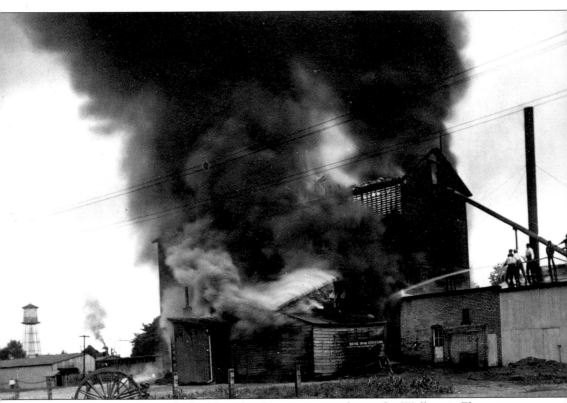

Fire fighters stand atop nearby buildings battling an intense fire at the Walkerton Elevator on September 7, 1913. (From the Collection of the Walkerton Historical Society.)

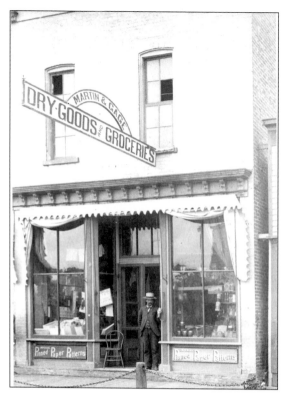

On February 18, 1891 the Martin and Gage Grocery Store opened in Walkerton. Standing in front of the store is the proprietor, Seth Martin. (From the Collection of the Walkerton Area Historical Society.)

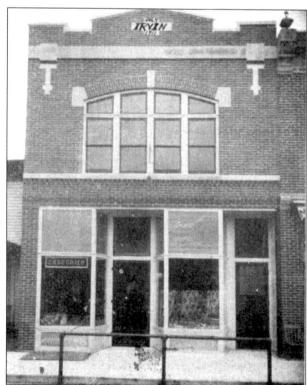

The Star Grocery Star in North Liberty is seen here as it appeared in 1911. (From the collection of the St. Joseph County Public Library.)

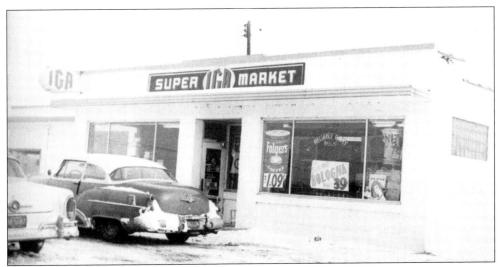

The corner of Mayflower and State Road 23 has proved successful for a country store. While it has changed names several times over the years, it remains the only grocery store in Greene Township. When this photograph was taken in 1962 the store was known as Mooney's IGA. (From the collection of the St. Joseph County Public Library.)

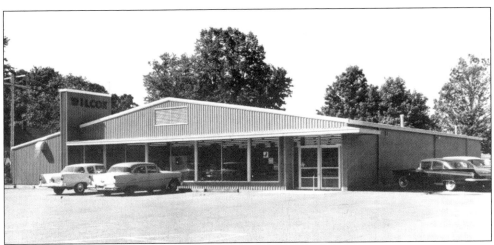

Brothers John and Roy Wilcox opened grocery stores in both North Liberty and Walkerton in the 1960s. The stores remained fixtures in both towns until the Five Store grocery chain purchased the stores in the early 1990s. Today, Dollar General Stores operate at both locations. Pictured here in 1962 is the North Liberty Wilcox store. (From the collection of the St. Joseph County Public Library.)

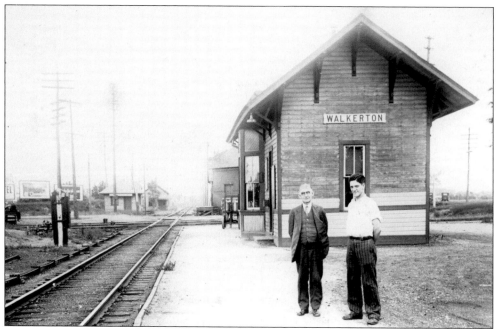

This Walkerton train depot was always a familiar landmark in the town of Walkerton. Standing in front of it are Joe Fitzgerald and A.J. Kennedy. (From the collection of the Walkerton Area Historical Society.)

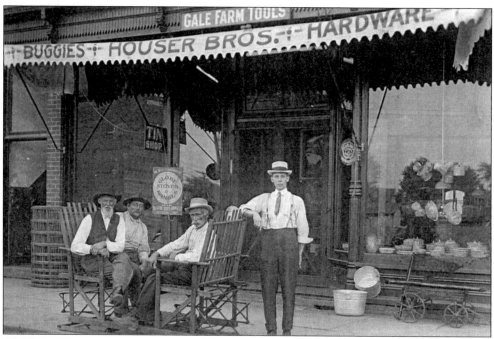

Claude E. Houser owned and operated the Houser Hardware Store in Walkerton from 1910–1961. Mr. Houser, who is standing in front of his store next to a group of unidentified men, also served a two-year term as sheriff of St. Joseph County in 1947 and served on both the school and library boards in Walkerton. (From the collection of the Walkerton Area Historical Society.)

Five

RELAXATION AND
RECREATION

"The bow cannot always stand bent, nor can human frailty subsist without some lawful recreation."
–Don Quixote, pt. I, IV, 21.

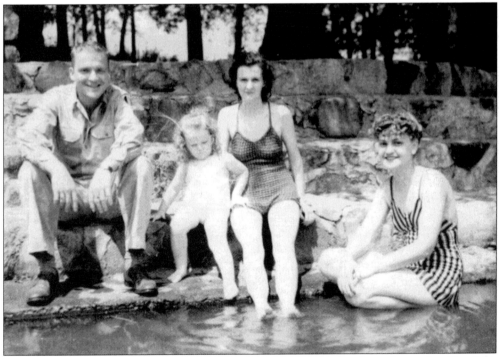

On furlough during World War II, a young G.I. relaxes with his family at the pool in City Park in North Liberty. Pictured, from left to right, are: Dale Nelson, Sandy Nelson, Irma Nelson, and Verla (Nelson) Burgener. (From the collection of the author.)

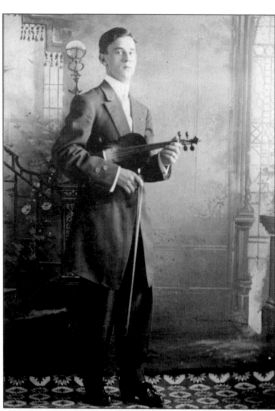

Posing with his violin is Vern Ake of Walkerton, c. 1895. (From the collection of the Walkerton Area Historical Society.)

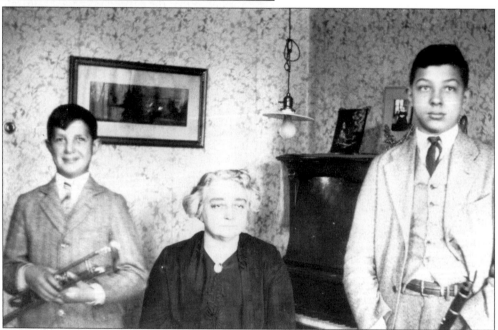

The Wolf trio, which was comprised of Addie Wolf and her nephews Ralph and Thomas Wolf, is seen here in 1928. The trio often played for round dances at the Gleaner Hall. (From the Collection of the Walkerton Area Historical Society.)

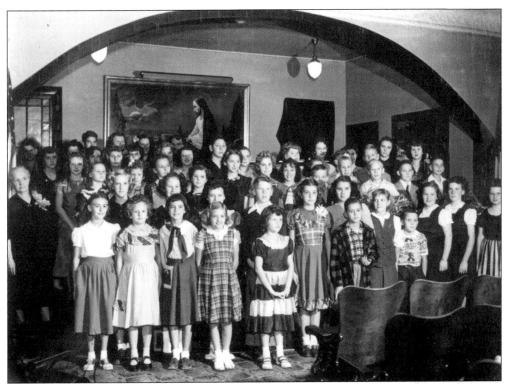

Pupils of Dora Steele, standing to the far left, participated in a piano recital at the First Brethren Church in North Liberty on Sunday October 23, 1949. (From the collection of the St. Joseph County Public Library.)

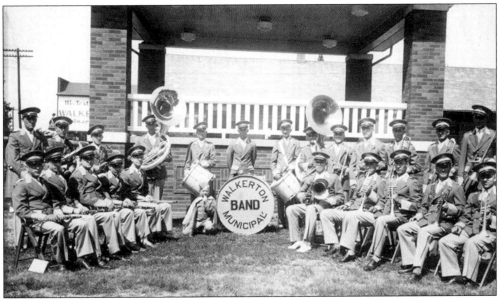

Comprised of town residents, the Walkerton Municipal Band is seen here *c.* 1935. (From the collection of the Walkerton Area Historical Society.)

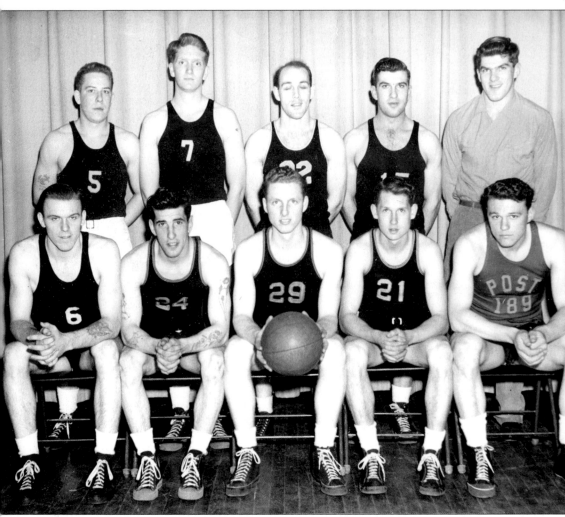

Many area merchants sponsored basketball teams in the 1940s, 1950s, and 1960s. The North Liberty Lumberyard sponsored one such team, the North Liberty Lumberjacks. The team was made up of former high school ball players, as well as returning servicemen. Pictured in this 1948 photograph, from left to right, are: (front row) John Markle, Bob Hostetler, Loren Knepp, Dick Adams, Don Daube; (back row) Rodger Reed, Dick Williams, Branson Hiatt, Herb Anderson, and Paul Anderson. (From the collection of Branson Hiatt.)

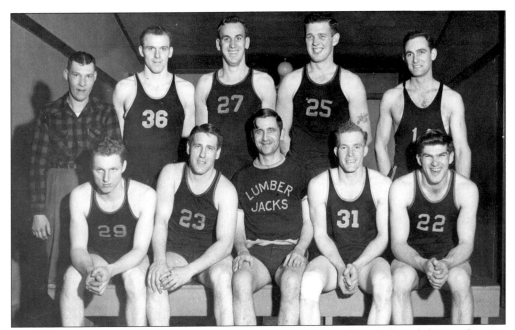

The Liberty Lumberjacks continued to play into the 1950s. Pictured, from left to right, are: (front row) Loren Knepp, Bill Hostetler, Coach John Chew, Harry Kane, Paul Anderson; (back row) Bernard Arnsberger, John Markle, Marion Frazer, Bob Folk, and unidentified. (From the collection of the Walkerton Area Historical Society.)

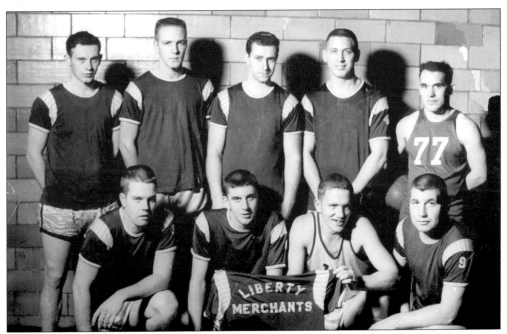

Several North Liberty merchants sponsored this basketball team in the early 1960s. Members of the Liberty Merchants team, pictured from left to right, are: (front row) Larry McDaniel, Chuck Yeager, Jerry Johnson, Damon Nichols; (back row) Johnny Carol, Roger Speir, Harold Kite, Bob Zellers, and Tom Miller. (From the collection of Bob Zellers.)

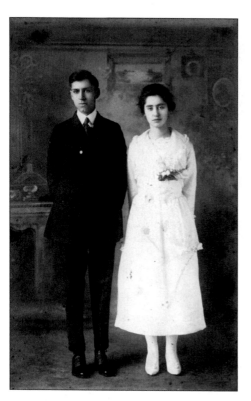

Wearing a typical wedding dress of the 1920s, the former Hazel Steele poses with her husband, George Clark. The wedding took place on January 12, 1921. (From the collection of Joyce Halt.)

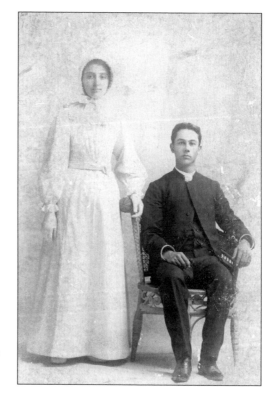

Pictured in their wedding photo are the former Lillie Clark and Merril I. Whitmer. Mr. and Mrs. Whitmer were married on September 20, 1896 in Liberty Township and wear attire associated with the Brethren Faith at that time. (From the collection of Debra Futa.)

Barely able to contain their joy, Lillie Pearl Kollar and Harrison Wade Hummer sit for their formal portrait of their January 20, 1903 wedding in Union Township. (From the collection of the author.)

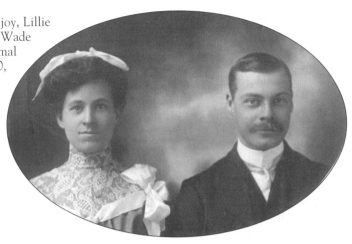

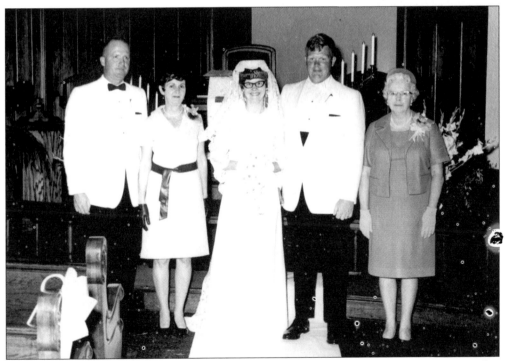

The support of one's family is always important when two people are united in marriage. Kathie Nelson and Dale Sheneman are shown with their parents after their wedding in the North Liberty United Methodist Church on September 14, 1968. Pictured, from left to right, are: Dale Nelson, Irma Nelson, Mrs. Sheneman, Mr. Sheneman, and Beatrice Sheneman. (From the collection of the author.)

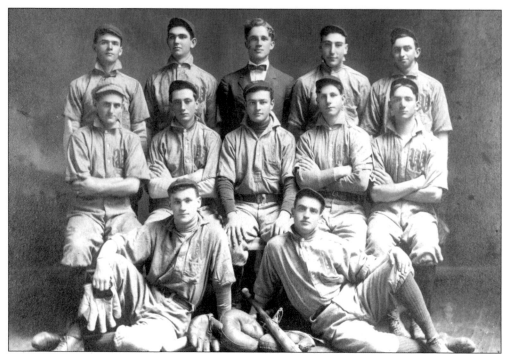

Winners of the 1911 St. Joseph County Baseball Championship were the Woodland Greys. Pictured, from left to right, are: (front row) E. Weber, C. Mochel; (second row) O. Kelley, D. Marker, O.J. Kelley, D. Flory, W. Geyer; (top row) H. Shearer, C. Shearer, H. Layer, J. Zeiger, and R. Kelley. (From the collection of Peggy Marker.)

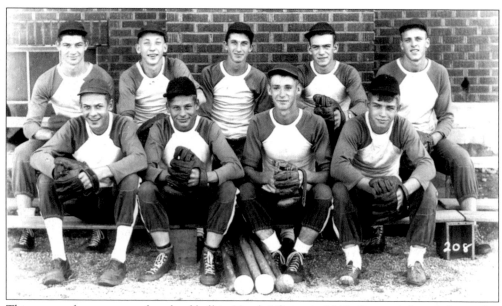

This group of young men played softball in North Liberty in 1947. Pictured, from left to right, are: (front row) Bob Hocker, John Holms, Maurice Liggett, Joe Kuff; (back row) Dallas Springman, Roger Reizer, Fred Anderson, Dale Gouker, and George Becktol. (From the collection of Maurice Liggett.)

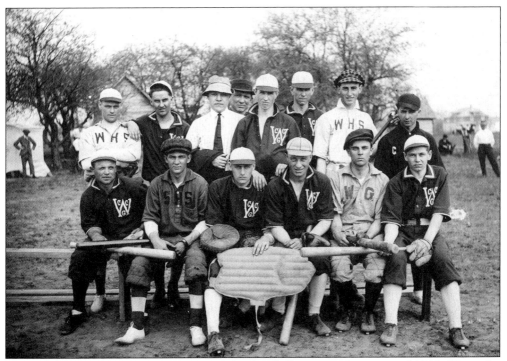

Walkerton's Cut Glass Factory sponsored this baseball team in the spring of 1915. (From the collection of the Walkerton Area Historical Society.)

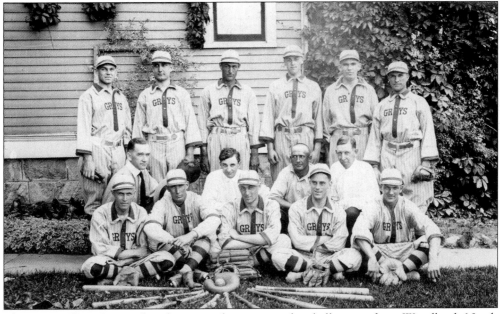

The name "Greys" proved to be a popular name as baseball teams from Woodland, North Liberty, and Walkerton were all named the "Greys." Pictured here are the Walkerton Greys c. 1915. (From the collection of the Walkerton Area Historical Society.)

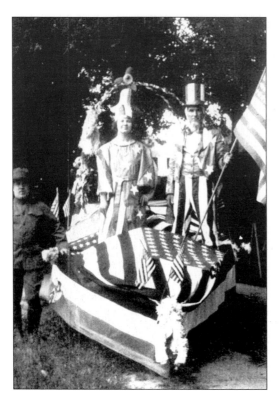

Patriotism comes naturally when "liberty" is part of your town's name. Riding atop the McDaniel Funeral Home float on July 4, 1928 are E.P. and Frances McDaniel. Mrs. McDaniel's brother, Fred Stedman, walks beside it. (From the collection of Donn McDaniel.)

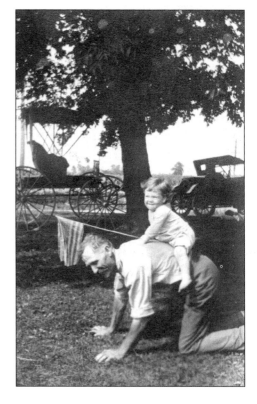

Picnics are always a favorite way to spend any summer holiday. And what better way to ride around than on Grandpa's back! Roscoe Turrell gives one of his grandchildren a ride in this July 4th photo c. 1920. (From the collection of the author.)

South Bend's mayor Lloyd Allen crowns Joyce McCormick of North Liberty the 1965 Christmas Seal Queen. (From the collection of the St. Joseph County Public Library.)

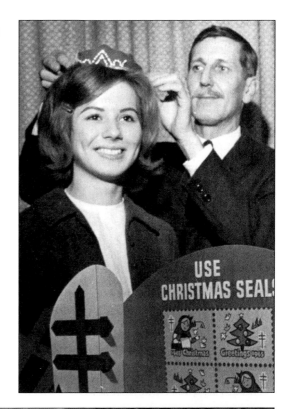

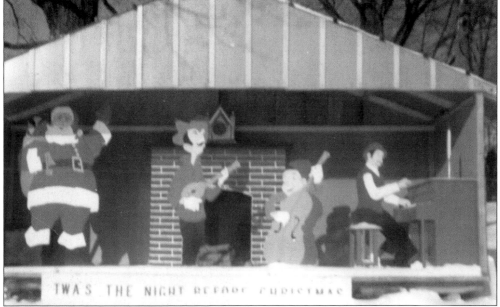

With over 1,000 lights and mechanical figures spread throughout the yard, people from all over would drive to see the elaborate Christmas displays at the home of Claude and Gladys Sheneman of North Liberty. Starting in the 1950s, Mr. and Mrs. Sheneman continued this tradition until they sold their home to make way for the Potato Creek State Park in the early 1970s. (From the collection of Gladys Sheneman.)

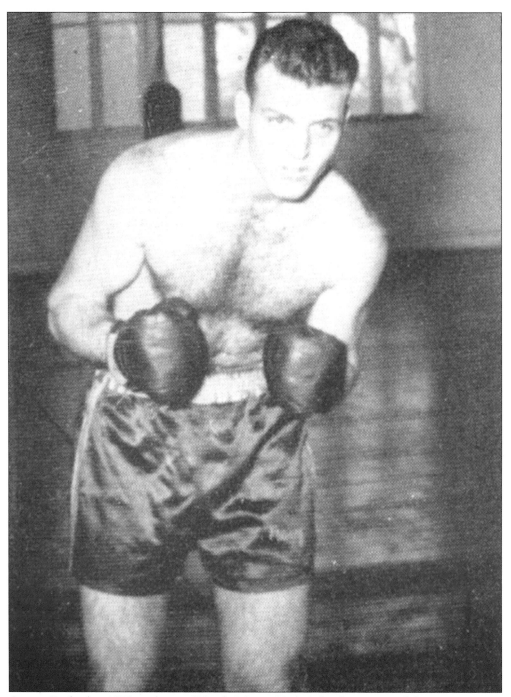

George Becktol, a 1950 graduate of North Liberty High School, was one of the nation's most outstanding amateur heavyweight boxers in the 1950s. As a member of the Great Lakes Navel Training Station's boxing team, Mr. Becktol won several championships, which prompted the U.S. Olympic team to ask him to take part in the 1952 Olympic trials. An illness forced him to miss the chance, but he continued to win fight after fight during his time with the Navy. (From the Collection of the St. Joseph County Public Library.)

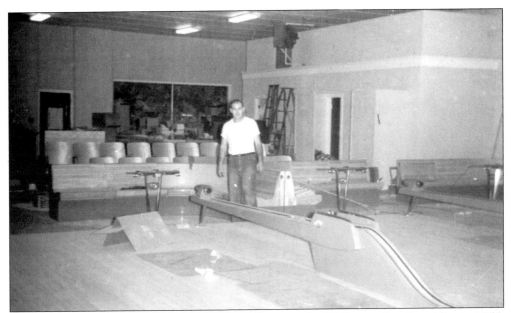

Bill Bouse converted the old Studebaker dealership into the Walkerton Bowling Alley in 1956. Mr. Bouse is seen here during construction of the alley. (From the collection of Bill Bouse.)

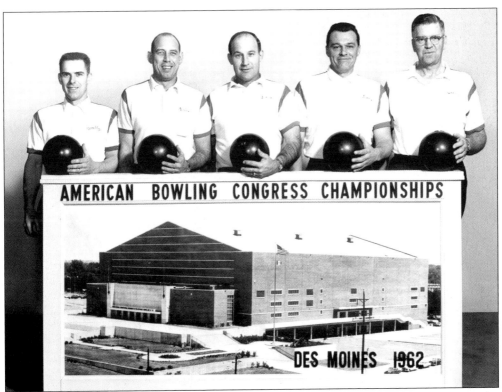

Members of this Walkerton Bowling team traveled to Des Moines, Iowa to compete in the national championship in 1962. Pictured, from left to right, are: Sonny Cripe, Bill Bouse, Bob Lute, Don Daube, and Albert Place. (From the collection of Bill Bouse.)

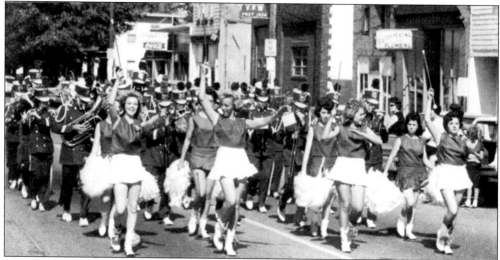

Whether marching in holiday parades or for homecoming festivities, the high school marching band has always put on a fantastic show for the crowds. Marching through North Liberty in the 1960s is the North Liberty High School Marching Band. (From the collection of the St. Joseph County Public Library.)

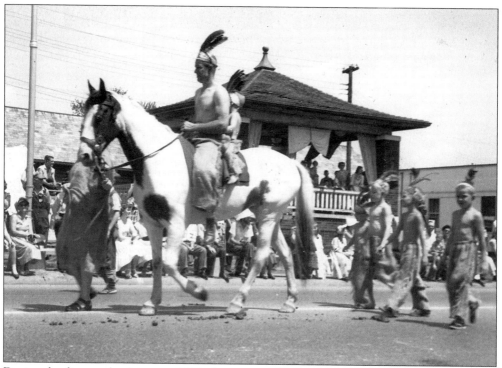

During the first week of August 1956, the town of Walkerton turned back the clocks with a huge centennial celebration. The highlight of the week took place on Saturday the 4th with a large parade through downtown. Commemorating the time when the Potawatomi Indians lived side by side with early settlers, this group proudly strolls by the happy spectators. (From the Collection of the Walkerton Area Historical Society.)

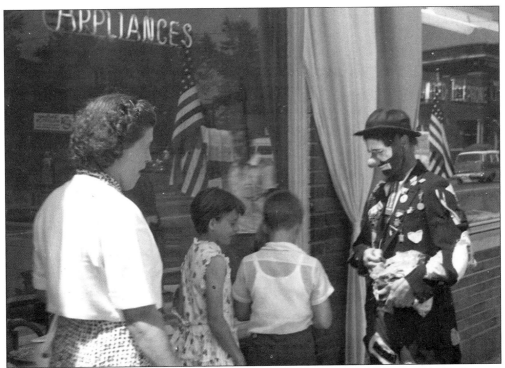

Two children enjoy the antics of a clown during the centennial celebration in Walkerton. (From the collection of the Walkerton Area Historical Society.)

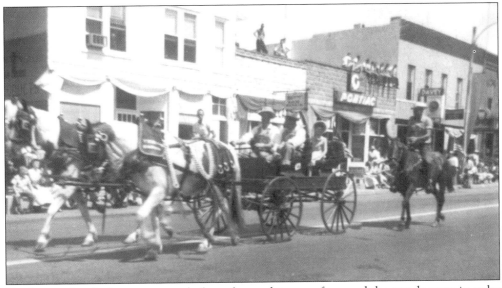

Hard pressed to find a seat, a crowd of people stand atop roofs around the parade route in order to enjoy the historic centennial parade. (From the collection of Kathie Sheneman.)

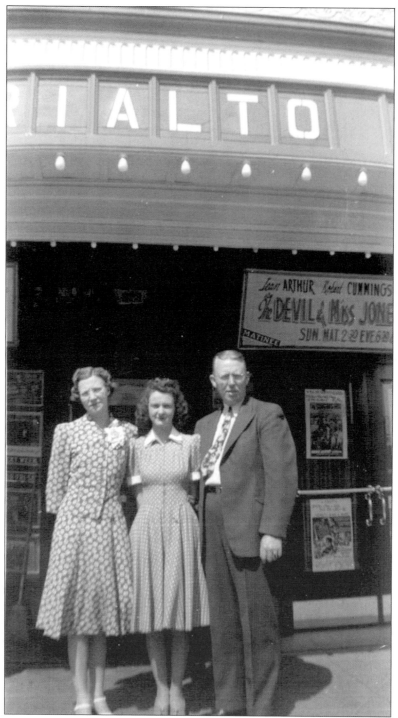

The Rialto Theater in Walkerton was a popular hangout for teens and families alike for the nearly 50 years it stood before being destroyed by fire in the early 1980s. The space where the theater once stood remains vacant to this day. Irma Walter, who was the popcorn popper, stands between owners Pearl and Jack Berglund in 1941. (From the collection of Irma Nelson.)

Six

CHURCH LIFE

"See, I lay a stone in Zion,
a tested stone,
a precious cornerstone for a sure foundation;
the one who trusts will never be dismayed."

–Isaiah 28, 16 NIV

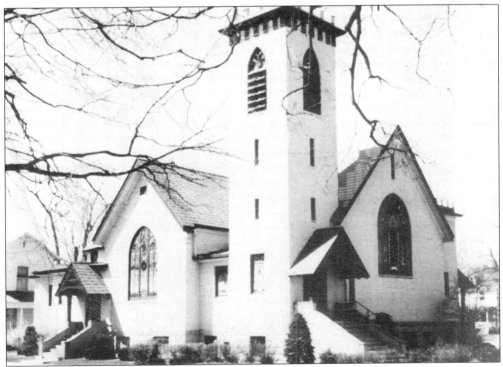

The North Liberty United Methodist Church, seen here in 1967, has the distinction of being the oldest Methodist Church to stay at the same location in all of Northern Indiana. The first church building was erected in 1851 and remained until the present sanctuary was built in 1912. (From the collection of Irma Nelson.)

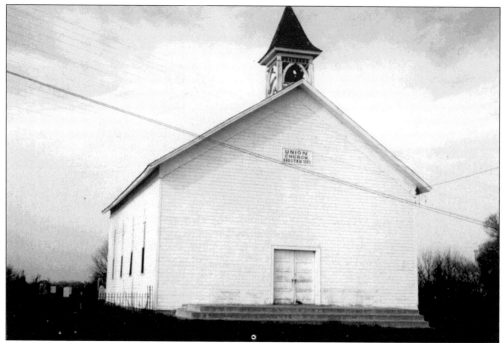

Pictured above is the Union Church located on Miami Road, between New and Osborn Roads in Union Township. The church stood from 1875 to 1964. (From the collection of Eileen Copsey.)

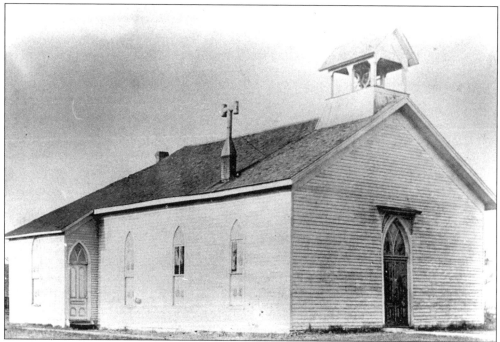

This building served as the Walkerton Methodist Episcopal Church until it was torn down in 1907 for the more modern church to be built. (From the collection of the Walkerton Area Historical Society.)

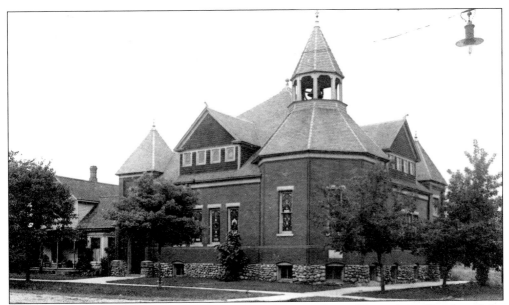

The Walkerton United Brethren Church *c.* 1915 is seen here. (From the collection of the Walkerton Area Historical Society.)

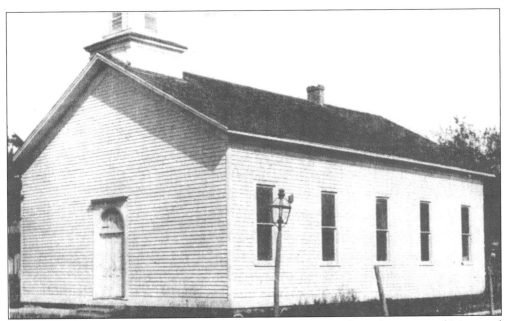

This building served as the Lakeville Christian Church, located on the corner of Main and Washington in Lakeville, from 1871 to 1919. (From the collection of Eileen Copsey.)

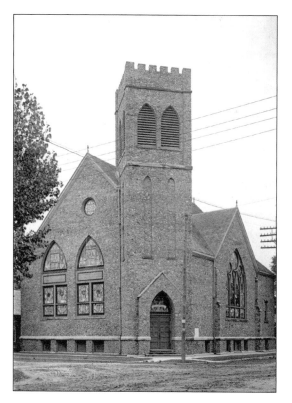

Erected in 1907, the Walkerton Methodist Episcopal Church was built from cobblestone gathered from nearby fields. (From the collection of the Walkerton Area Historical Society.)

Presumably started from space heaters used the night before at a chicken pie supper, the Walkerton Methodist Episcopal Church burned to the ground the morning of February 20, 1936. (From the collection of the Walkerton Area Historical Society.)

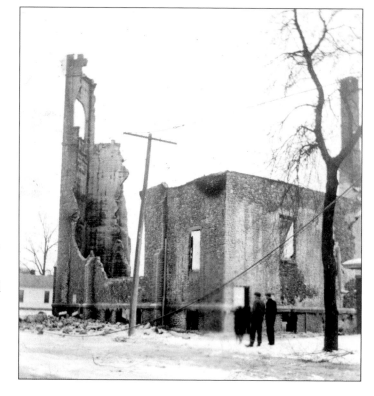

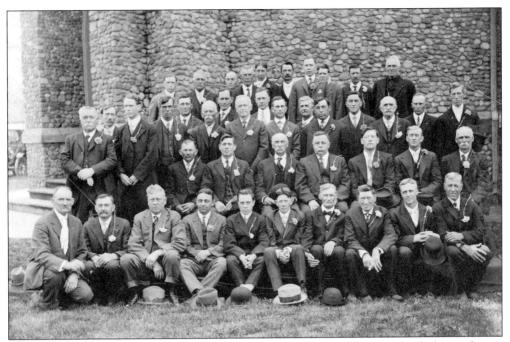

Members of the Walkerton Methodist Episcopal Church men's Sunday school class gather in front of the church c. 1916. (From the collection of the Walkerton Area Historical Society.)

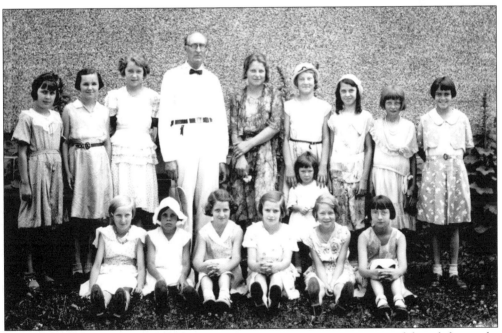

The Lakeville Christian Church Sunday School class of the 1930s, pictured from left to right includes: (front row) Eileen Kline, Alice Deal, Marjorie Plummer, Betty Barkley, Betty Berry, Jackie Wickharn; (back row) Jean Grof, Glee Herbster, Virginia Berry, Reverend Wickhorn, Betty Sheneman, Connie Weaver, (?) Weaver, Irene Berger, Clara Hertel, Mary Alice Plummer. (From the collection of Eileen Copsey.)

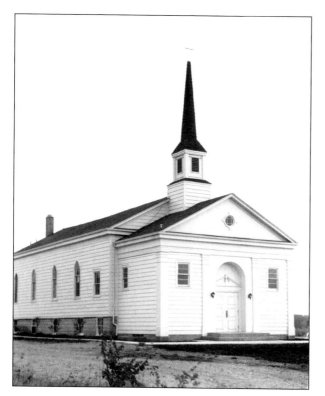

At one time part of the German Reformed Church, the St. Johns Lutheran Church has had a long history dating back to the 1860s. The church, located on Riley Road, is seen here *c*. 1960. (From the collection of the author.)

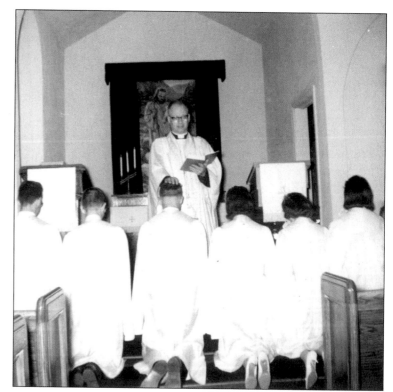

Rev. John Wesley Hanson confirms a group of young adults into the St. Johns Lutheran Church on April 22, 1962. (From the collection of the author.)

St. Philip's Church was located east of North Liberty and is seen here in 1875. Surnames of those that attended the church include: Carr, Roysden, Stevenson, Gushwa, McKenzie, Pearse, Plagler, Rupel, and Rowan. (From the collection of the St. Joseph County Public Library.)

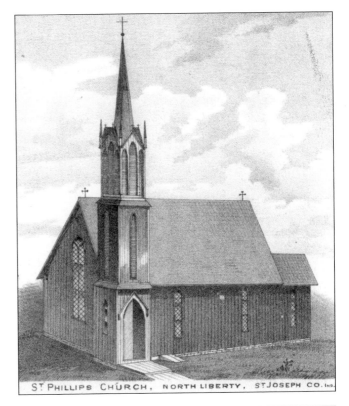

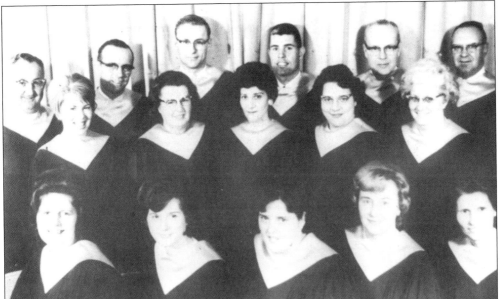

The 1967 North Liberty United Methodist Church choir pictured, from left to right, includes: (front row) Becky Burch, Karen McCormick, Betty Peddycord, Elta Steele, Zelpha Walsh; (second row) Nancy Mangus, Lela Fisher, Madelyn Nelson, Elaine Wagner, Caroline Shupert; (back row) Bill Hartman, Ozzie Fisher, Rev. Tom Frost, Forrest Dunnuck, Max Steele, and Chester Walter. (From the Collection of Irma Nelson.)

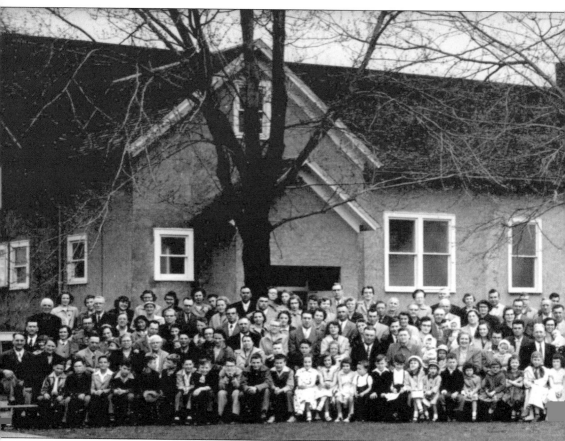

The Pine Creek Church of the Brethren was one of four Brethren Churches located in Southern St. Joseph County. Ministers would preach one Sunday a month at each of the four locations. The Pine Creek house of worship was known as the East House until officially changing its name to the Pine Creek Church of the Brethren around 1917. The original church, located on the corners of Stanton and Pine Roads, stood across from where the currant church stands today. Surnames of the families who appear in this 1954 photograph are: Fish,

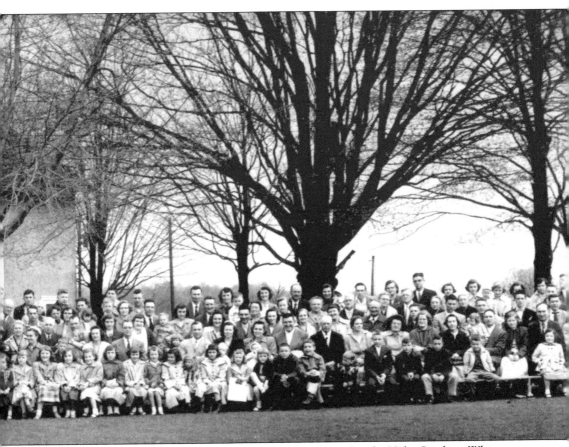

Stump, Kranitz, Clark, Mueller, Baughman, Freeman, Buss, Smith, Halt, Sanders, Whitmer, Stull, Houser, Rowe, Johnson, Ross, Zehner, Herbster, Weigand, Lasmanis, Roush, Wort, Burke, Koenig, Holland, Traux, Danner, Platz, Gerdes, Gensinger, McBride, Dolph, Rupel, Lehman, Hartsough, Balsbaugh, Culp, Longenecker, Keiser, Augh, Hoover, Hepler, Freeman, Goon, Peters, Eslinger, Lasmanis, Danner, Zehner, Naragon, Gardner, Six, and Wort (From the collection of Joyce Halt.)

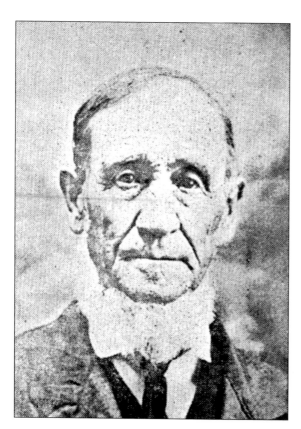

Known as Uncle Sammy to the residents of Greene Township, Rev. Samuel Rupe was one of the first Methodist ministers in this county. Though he was quite deaf and carried a tin ear trumpet, many pioneer residents would recall the fervor with which his cracked voice raised when signing "A Charge to Keep I Have." Reverend Rupe passed away in 1885. (From the collection of Verla Burgener.)

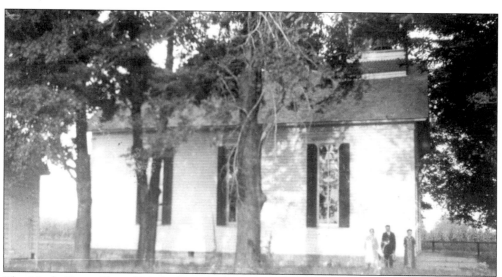

The Maple Grove United Methodist Church, located on the corner of New and Maple Roads, had its beginnings as a prayer group in the Hummer Schoolhouse. As the congregation grew services were held in the nearby Olive Branch Brethren Church. In 1878, John Hummer donated a portion of his farmland so that the present sanctuary could be built. (From the collection of the author.)

Seven
CEMETERIES

"To die, to sleep; to sleep perchance to dream."

–Hamlet 3:1, 65-66

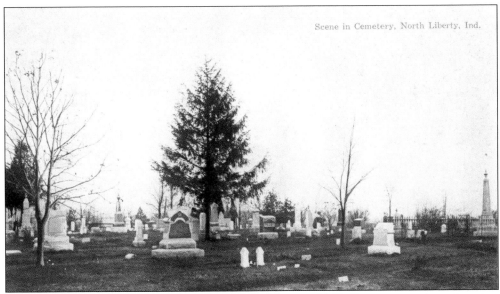

East Lawn Cemetery in North Liberty is pictured here *c.* 1917. Gravestones show that the cemetery has been used since at least 1842. (From the collection of the author.)

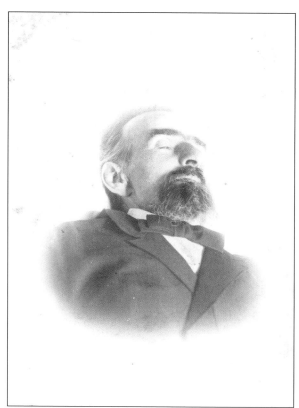

Photographers often showed up at the homes of grieving families to photograph the dead. This came as a blessing to those families whose loved one was never photographed in life. John Walter was one such "customer." Mr. Walter passed away on December 4, 1896. (From the collection of the author.)

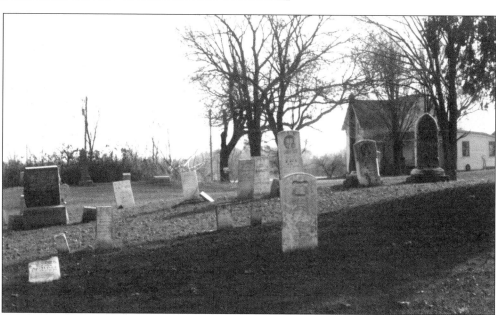

The Dice Cemetery, located on the corners of Oak and Riley Roads, was first used as a cemetery when two children of Benjamin Dice were buried there on the same day in 1850. For nearly 100 years, pioneer families that lived around the area buried their dead in this remote cemetery in Union Township. (From the collection of the author.)

Keeping a cemetery in tip-top shape falls on the shoulders of the sexton. From 1934 to 1964, Ernest Finch, seen here in 1953, was the sexton of Sumption Prairie Cemetery. Other sextons of the cemetery have included Peter Reaves and Henry Miller. (From the collection of the late Ruth Finch.)

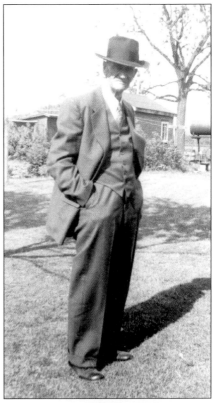

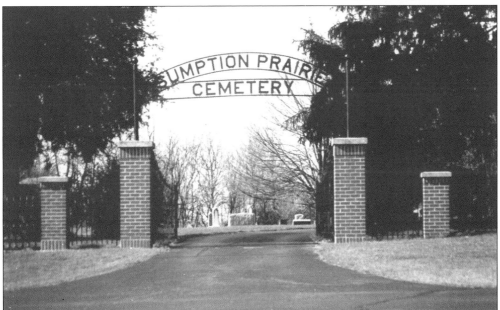

The first burial in Sumption Prairie, located on the corners of Kern and Sumption Trail, took place in January of 1833 when Isaac Rudduck was laid to rest. Rudduck was the first pioneer resident to die in Greene Township. The fence that borders the cemetery was once used around the old courthouse in South Bend and was purchased in 1896. (From the collection of the author.)

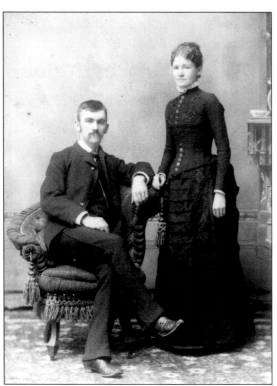

The undertaker for the town of Walkerton in the 1890s was Harvey Albert Yearrick. The funeral profession proved popular as two of Mr. Yearrick's nephews, Harry L. Yearrick and Howard J. Hummer became well known undertakers in later years. Pictured with Mr. Yearrick c. 1895 is his wife Nancy Ellen Hummer. (From the collection of Jeannette Hummer.)

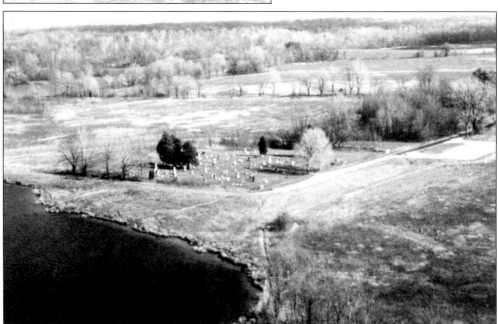

The Porter-Rea Cemetery, located in Potato Creek State Park, was recognized in the fall of 2003 for its historical significance to the area. As the historic marker reads, "free African-American Settlers from the Huggart Settlement were buried here alongside their white neighbors, not segregated." The cemetery, whose burials date back to the 1850s, is seen here in an aerial view. (From the Collection of Potato Creek State Park.)

This ad for the McDaniel Funeral Home advertises both undertaking and ambulance services. (From the collection of Gladys Albright.)

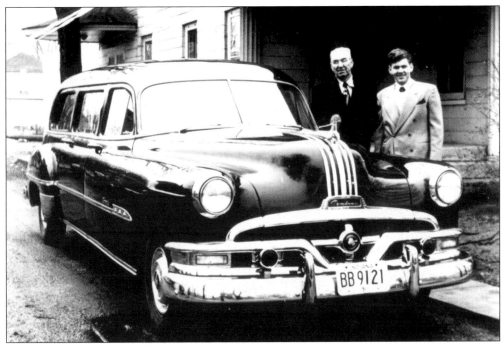

All it took for this automobile to go from an ambulance to a hearse was the changing of the curtains in the window! Pictured with funeral director E.P. McDaniel is his son Donn in the late 1940s. (From the collection of Donn McDaniel.)

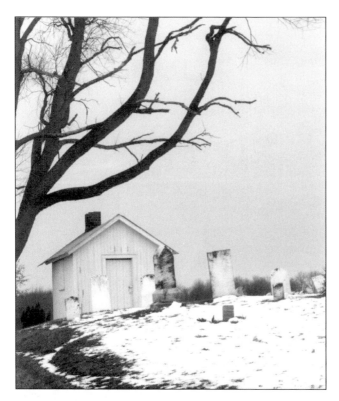

John McMillen donated a portion of his land in 1852 for the Fair Cemetery to be created. It is the final resting place for many pioneer families. Surnames of some of these families include: Mangus, Kneep, Fair, Houser, Kaser, Clark, and Stump. It is located on the corner of Oak and Stanton Roads. (From the collection of the author.)

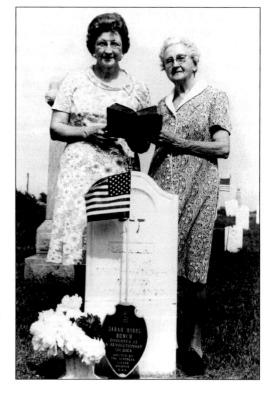

Sarah Hobbs Bunch, who passed away in 1875, was honored in the 1960s with a plaque at her gravestone indicating that she was the daughter of a Revolutionary War solider. Mrs. Bunch's great granddaughter, Florence (Bunch) Kline, on the right, stands with a member of the Schulyer Colfax Chapter of the D.A.R. at the gravesite of Mrs. Bunch at the Lakeville Cemetery. (From the collection of Eileen Copsey.)

Eight
NOW AND THEN

"O! Call back yesterday, bid time return."

–King Richard II, 3:2, 69

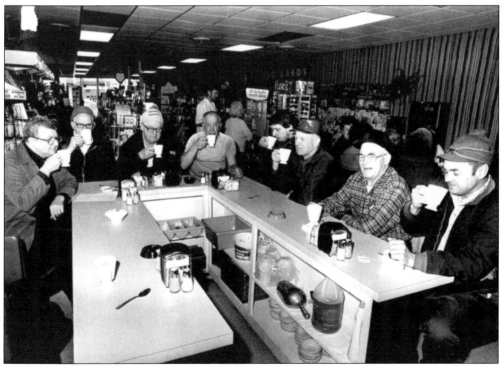

Whether discussing world politics or simply reminiscing about the past, wherever coffee is being served, citizens will gather. Conjugating for coffee in Jacobs Drugstore in North Liberty in the winter of 1980 are, from left to right: Rev. Gaylord Saltzgaber, Barney Wentz, Cecil Weber, Virgil Robinson, Bruce Weber, Lyle McCormick, Harvey Whitmer, and Roger Morris. (From the collection Pam Craft.)

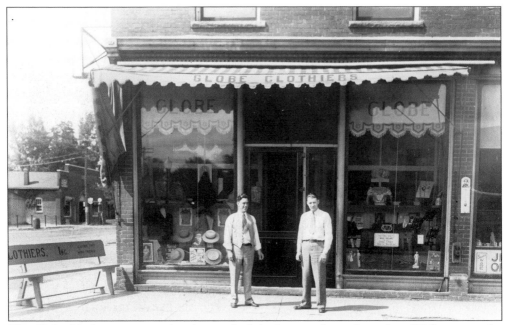

The Globe Clothers store was the place to find the latest styles and trends in Walkerton in the 1920s. The store was owned by Vern Gindelberger and was located on the corner of Roosevelt and Illinois Street. Standing in front of the store is Vern Ake and Roy Gindelberger. (From the collection of the Walkerton Area Historical Society.)

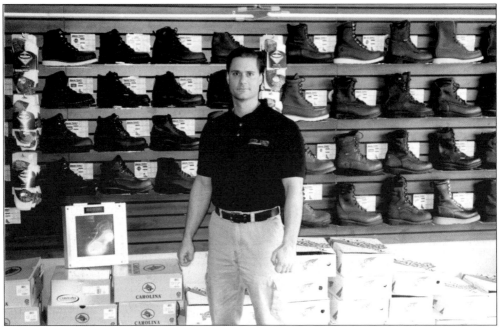

In August of 1995, Working Persons Shoes opened its doors on U.S. 31 in Lakeville by father and son team Dennis and Eric Deniger. The store specializes in quality work clothing and footwear. Pictured in front of the many styles of shoes and boots is Eric Deniger. (From the collection of the author.)

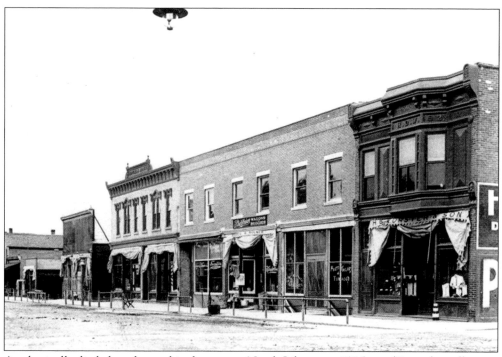

Aesthetically, little has changed in downtown North Liberty, c. 1915 . . . (From the collection of Bob's Country Store; North Liberty.)

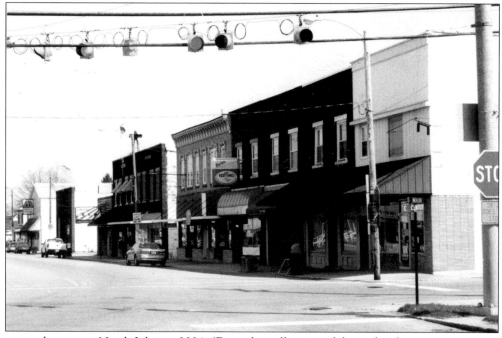

. . . to downtown North Liberty, 2004. (From the collection of the author.)

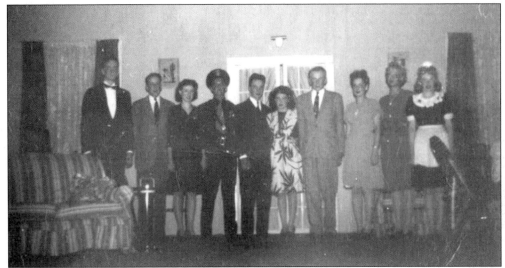

Members of the North Liberty High School class of 1947 senior play, *Alibi Bill*, pictured from left to right, are: Dick Williams, John Stump, Dorothy Allriedge, Dick Jones, Jack Farrar, Fauntelle McDaniel, Jim Williams, Vona Summers, unidentified, and Mardell Ross. (From the collection of Fauntelle Spellman.)

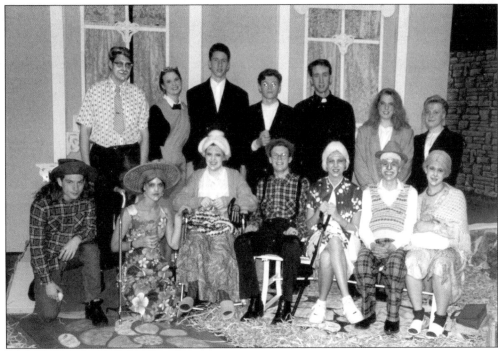

With the help of some make up and wigs, the cast members of *The Silver Whistle* went from teenagers to octogenarians. Pictured in this 1993 John Glenn production, from left to right, are: (front row) Shawn Correll, Beth Thomas, Becca VanWechel, Frank Sheneman, Gwen Kelley, Barry Houser, Kelley Tingle; (back row) Keith Anderson, Aimee Christensen, Russell Burch, Chad Hostetler, Jay Cotton, Laura Bostwick, and Kelley Stedman. (From the collection of Barry's Photography; LaPorte Indiana.)

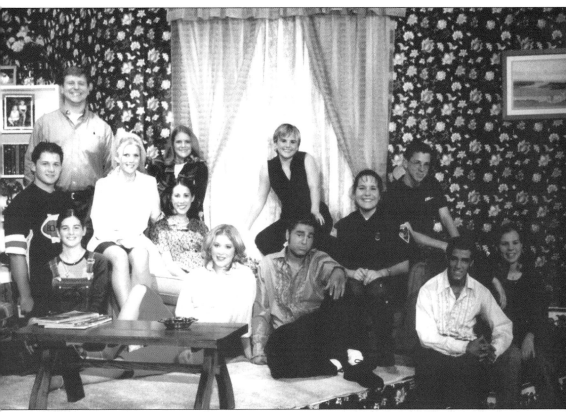

For over a decade, Richard Fansler has brought his extraordinary directing skills to the stage of John Glenn High School. After each production students are left with a greater appreciation of the theater and with the knowledge that they will forever be one of "Fansler's Kids." Pictured in the 1999 production of *The Odd Couple*, from left to right, are: (front row) Stephanie Drotar, Jenna Pace, Chris Keck, Cory Miller, Adalee Pairitz; (second row) Ryan Austin, Olivia Bellinger, Emily Batman, Jaymie Baker; (back row) Mr. Fansler, Mollie Pletcher, Melissa Ganser, and Brian Hulse. (From the collection of Barry's Photography; LaPorte, Indiana.)

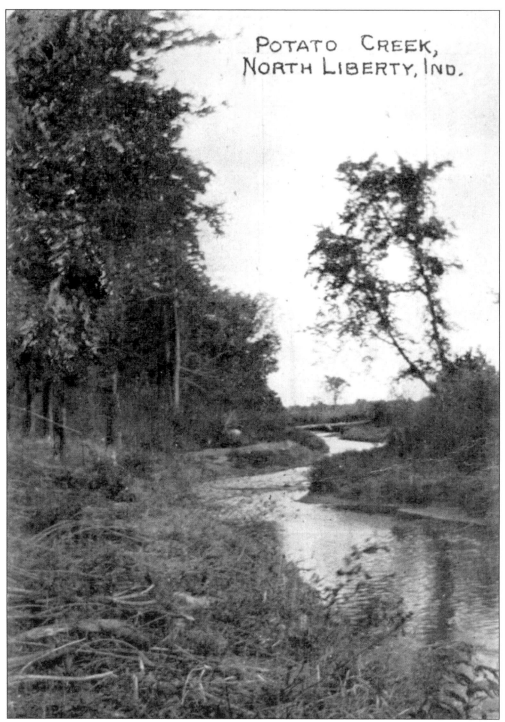

From mills that were powered by its water, to the park that bares its name, Potato Creek has had a major impact in the southern part of the county. Early pioneer baptisms, as well as recreational past times such as skinny dipping and fishing have all been a part of the creeks history. Potato Creek is seen here *c.* 1915. (From the collection of Toni Cook.)

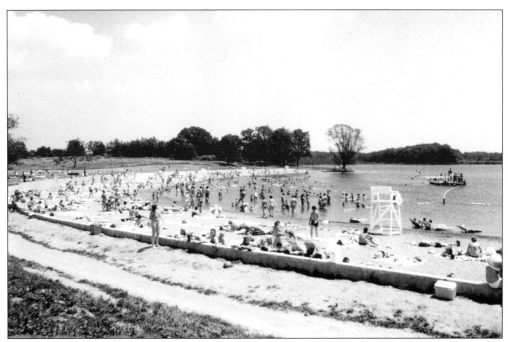

Worster Lake, located in Potato Creek State Park, was named for Darcy Worster who was a naturalist and an early park supporter. Besides fishing and boating, the beach at Worster Lake is a popular summer location. (From the collection of Potato Creek State Park.)

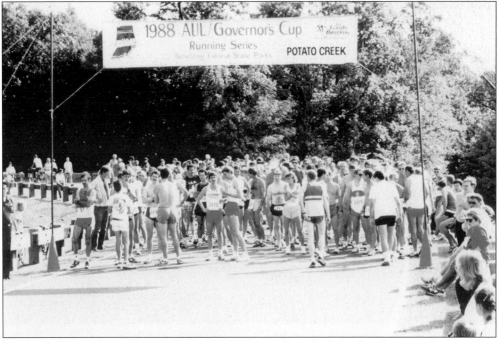

Besides fishing, hiking, and camping, Potato Creek State Park is also the site of many other outdoor activities including the AUE/Governors Cup Race. Racers gather at the starting point of the race in 1988. (From the Collection of the Potato Creek State Park.)

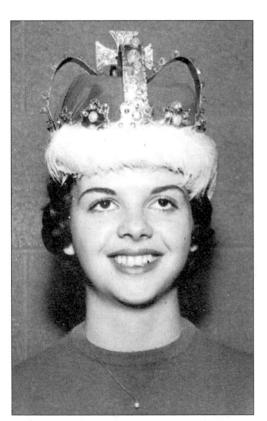

One of the happiest times of the school year is the week of homecoming. Decorations adorn shop windows, parades are held, and the big game is played. One of the most anticipated events of the week is the crowing of the homecoming royalty. Gloria Nelson beams from ear to ear as she is crowned the 1961 North Liberty High School Football Homecoming queen. (From the Collection of Gloria Kranitz.)

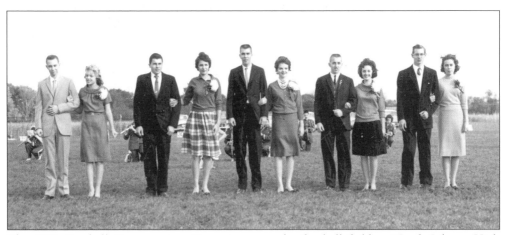

The 1961 Football Homecoming Court poses on the football field at North Liberty High School. (From the collection of Gloria Kranitz.)

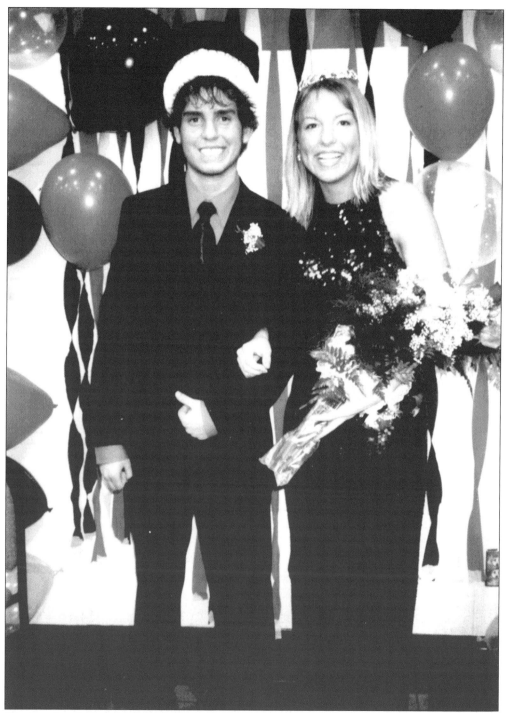

Proving that high school traditions transcend the test of time, Adam Rodriguez and Sarah Keeling are crowned the 2003 John Glenn High School Basketball Homecoming King and Queen. (From the Collection of the *Walkerton Herald*.)

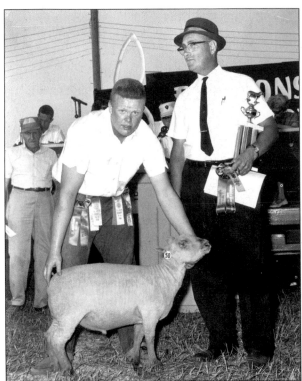

Dale Sheneman of Liberty Township holds his 110-pound crossbreed sheep that won the grand champion ribbon at the St. Joseph County 4-H Fair in August of 1964. (From the Collection of Kathie Sheneman.)

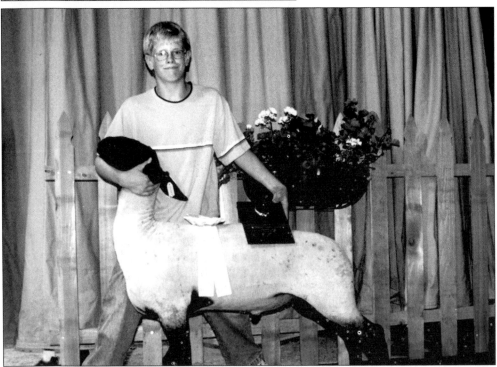

Justin Podell, of Union Township, poses with his reserve grand champion sheep at the 2002 St. Joseph County 4-H Fair. (From the collection of Rick Podell.)

Gary Troust and Tom McGee, members of the 1969 John Glenn High School Basketball team, try to steal the ball from a member of the rival Knox squad. The 1968–1969 school year was the first year the Falcons played in their new gym in Walkerton. (From the collection of the Walkerton-Lincoln Township Public Library.)

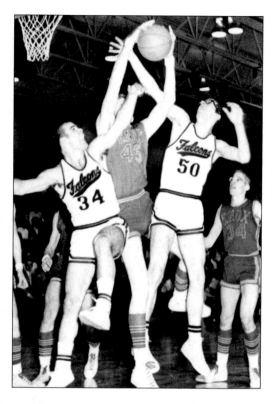

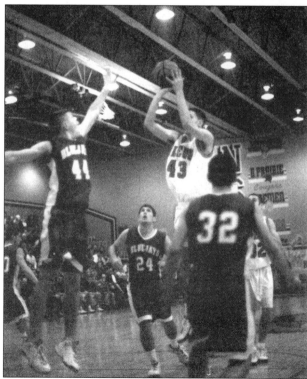

Matt Jerrell of John Glenn shoots for two during a game in 2001. (From the collection of the John Glenn High School.)

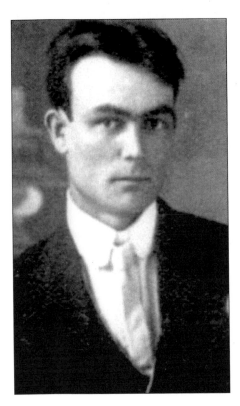

From chasing rowdy kids who stole watermelons out of town, to keeping the peace when neighbors got into a dispute, order was maintained in North Liberty by town marshal Earl Bulla in the 1940s. (From the collection of Barbara Blair.)

St. Joseph County lost one of their finest on December 13, 2003 when Officer Bryan Verkler, a 1994 graduate of John Glenn High School, was tragically killed in the line of duty serving as a patrolman for the Mishawka Police Department. During the eulogy at the funeral Mishawaka Mayor Robert Beutter perfectly summed up the man Bryan was, "Giant in size, giant in strength, giant in heart, giant in pride, giant in valor, giant in sacrifice!" (From the collection of Randy and Carolyn Verkler.)

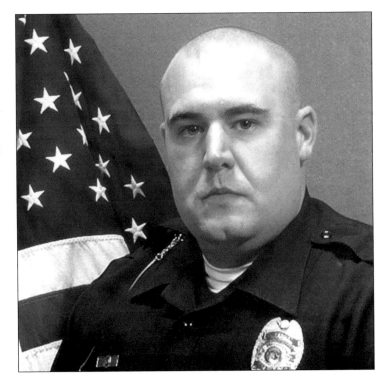